We Sang in Hushed Voices

THE AZRIELI SERIES OF HOLOCAUST SURVIVOR MEMOIRS: PREVIOUSLY PUBLISHED TITLES

We Sang in Hushed Voices

Helena Jockel

THE AZRIELI FOUNDATION
www.azrielifoundation.org

Cover and book design by Mark Goldstein
Endpaper maps by Martin Gilbert
Map on page xxvii by François Blanc
Cover photo by Matias Kallio
Family tree on pages xxviii–xxix by Keaton Taylor.
Photos on page 83 courtesy of Ghetto Fighters' House Museum.
Photo 1 on page 85 courtesy of the United States Holocaust Memorial Museum.

LIBRARY AND ARCHIVES CANADA CATALOGUING IN PUBLICATION

Jockel, Helena, 1919–
     We sang in hushed voices/ Helena Jockel.

(The Azrieli series of Holocaust survivor memoirs; VI)
Includes bibliographical references and index.
ISBN 978-1-897470-43-5 (pbk.)

1. Jockel, Helena, 1919–. 2. Holocaust, Jewish (1939–1945) – Czechoslovakia – Personal narratives. 3. Holocaust, Jewish (1939–1945) – Poland – Personal narratives. 4. Jews – Czechoslovakia – Biography. 5. Holocaust survivors – Canada – Biography. 6. Czechoslovakia – Biography. I. Azrieli Foundation, issuing body II. Title. III. Series: Azrieli series of Holocaust survivor memoirs. Series; VI

DS135.C97J63 2014   940.53'18092   C2014-901193-8

MIX
From responsible sources
FSC   FSC® C004191
www.fsc.org

PRINTED IN CANADA

The Azrieli Series of Holocaust Survivor Memoirs

Contents

Series Preface:
In their own words. . .

In telling these stories, the writers have liberated themselves. For so many years we did not speak about it, even when we became free people living in a free society. Now, when at last we are writing about what happened to us in this dark period of history, knowing that our stories will be read and live on, it is possible for us to feel truly free. These unique historical documents put a face on what was lost, and allow readers to grasp the enormity of what happened to six million Jews – one story at a time.

David J. Azrieli, C.M., C.Q., M.Arch
Holocaust survivor and founder, The Azrieli Foundation

Since the end of World War II, over 30,000 Jewish Holocaust survivors have immigrated to Canada. Who they are, where they came from, what they experienced and how they built new lives for themselves and their families are important parts of our Canadian heritage. The Azrieli Foundation's Holocaust Survivor Memoirs Program was established to preserve and share the memoirs written by those who survived the twentieth-century Nazi genocide of the Jews of Europe and later made their way to Canada. The program is guided by the conviction that each survivor of the Holocaust has a remarkable story to tell, and that such stories play an important role in education about tolerance and diversity.

Millions of individual stories are lost to us forever. By preserving the stories written by survivors and making them widely available to a broad audience, the Azrieli Foundation's Holocaust Survivor Memoirs Program seeks to sustain the memory of all those who perished at the hands of hatred, abetted by indifference and apathy. The personal accounts of those who survived against all odds are as different as the people who wrote them, but all demonstrate the courage, strength, wit and luck that it took to prevail and survive in such terrible adversity. The memoirs are also moving tributes to people – strangers and friends – who risked their lives to help others, and who, through acts of kindness and decency in the darkest of moments, frequently helped the persecuted maintain faith in humanity and courage to endure. These accounts offer inspiration to all, as does the survivors' desire to share their experiences so that new generations can learn from them.

The Holocaust Survivor Memoirs Program collects, archives and publishes these distinctive records and the print editions are available free of charge to libraries, educational institutions and Holocaust-education programs across Canada. They are also available for sale to the general public at bookstores.

The Azrieli Foundation would like to express appreciation to the following people for their invaluable efforts in producing this book: Carolyn Ferstman Condé, Sherry Dodson (Maracle Press), Sir Martin Gilbert, Jana Jockel, Pavel Jockel, Matias Kallio, Farla Klaiman, Zvika Oren from the Ghetto Fighters' House Museum, Mia Spiro, Keaton Taylor, Caroline Waddell of the US Holocaust Memorial Museum, and Margie Wolfe and Emma Rodgers of Second Story Press.

About the Glossary

The following memoir contains a number of terms, concepts and historical references that may be unfamiliar to the reader. For information on major organizations; significant historical events and people; geographical locations; religious and cultural terms; and foreign-language words and expressions that will help give context and background to the events described in the text, please see the glossary beginning on page 67.

Introduction

"I still believe that people are really good at heart"
– Helena Jockel's journey.

When Helena Jockel begins her memoir with a chapter entitled "My Mukačevo" she is not referring to yet another dot on a variegated map of Europe. This is the town where Helena was born – what she calls "my" place – the memory of which still tugs at her heartstrings. A hundred and thirty kilometres east of Mukačevo lies Sighet, a town in present-day Romania, which is the birthplace of Nobel Peace Prize laureate and Holocaust survivor Elie Wiesel. Just a little further is Czernovitz, in present-day Ukraine, where Paul Celan, another Holocaust survivor and the greatest contemporary poet of the German language, penned his first poems. Yet despite its illustrious sons, we know very little about Jewish life in this remote part of Eastern Europe, tucked between the Carpathian Mountains and the Hungarian plains. The first chapters of Helena's memoir give us a precious glimpse into that life.

Lying directly at the juncture of several countries, the Subcarpathian region was ruled by a succession of governments, and the changes are reflected in the variety of its place names. One of the scholars researching the region cites the following humorous quotation:

It is possible to:
Have been born in Austria-Hungary,
Have been married in Czechoslovakia,
Have given birth in Hungary,
Have lived with your family in the Soviet Union,
Reside currently in Ukraine ...
And never have left the city of Mukacheve.[1]

Helena's Mukačevo was called Munkács in Hungarian and Mukachevo (Мукачево) in Ukrainian. In the second half of the nineteenth century, Subcarpathia belonged to the Austro-Hungarian Empire, but, after World War I and the Peace Treaty of Versailles, it became part of the newly created country of Czechoslovakia. Following Adolf Hitler's rise to power, Mukačevo was annexed by Hungary, an ally of Nazi Germany, as a result of the 1938 Munich Agreement. [2] In 1944, Germany broke off its pact with Hungary and invaded the country and all the territories under its rule. Within three months, all of the Subcarpathian region was made *judenrein* (free of Jews).[3] After

---

1 Anna Berger, *Munkács: A Jewish World That Was.* An M.A thesis for the Department of Hebrew, Biblical and Jewish Studies, the University of Sydney, 2009. Accessed at http://ses.library.usyd.edu.au//bitstream/2123/6336/4/berger_thesis_2009. pdf on January 10, 2014.

2 In 1938, Germany, United Kingdom, France, and Italy signed a settlement that permitted Nazi Germany to annex portions of Czechoslovakia (which were then named Sudetenland). The agreement was negotiated in Munich without Czechoslovakia's presence. The pact was an unsuccessful attempt to appease Germany's expansionist designs.

3 See http://www.yadvashem.org/yv/en/exhibitions/communities/munkacs/overview.asp>. See also Yeshayahu A. Jelinek, *The Carpathian Diaspora: The Jews of the Subcarpathian Rus' and Mukachevo, 1848–1948* (|East European Monographs, New York: Columbia University Press, 2007), and Raz Segal, *Days of Ruin: The Jews of Munkács during the Holocaust* (Jerusalem: Yad Vashem, 2013).

the war, the territory was included in the Ukrainian part of the Soviet Union and was Russianized. Today, Helena's hometown is a city in southwestern Ukraine, and very few Jews live there now. The entire Jewish way of life in the region is no more.

Before the war, Mukačevo was home to the largest Jewish community in Subcarpathia. Established in the first half of the eighteenth century, it boasted synagogues, schools, printing presses and other institutions that helped foster a rich and vibrant Jewish culture. The Jews of Mukačevo contributed to the colourful social fabric of the town and comprised a spectrum of social and religious mores, professions, levels of education and political affiliations. On the eve of World War II, many were deeply religious *Hasidim*, led by the ultra-Orthodox rabbis who favoured isolation from the rest of the world. At the same time, the number of Jews who embraced modernization, Zionism and assimilation was growing, and a high percentage of the intelligentsia, professionals and artists were Jewish. Some were social reformers and others joined clandestine political organizations, such as Helena's older brother, Chaim, who became a member of the outlawed Communist Party. Helena's mother, kind and open-minded, favoured social change and strongly supported her children's aspirations for secular learning.

Helena describes Mukačevo as a multicultural and religious mosaic, with Jews (who made up more than 40 per cent of its population of 20,000), Carpatho-Ruthenians, Magyars, Ukrainians, Roma, Czechs, Slovaks, Poles and Germans living side by side in relative harmony. Today, the only traces of this polyglot mix can be found in expatriate places such as Helena's living room in Halifax, Nova Scotia, where she effortlessly switches from Czech to Hungarian to Russian, though she is also fluent in German, Hebrew and English. During the Holocaust, this ability to communicate in different languages was a major factor in Helena's survival.

Helena's parents owned a bakery, though it was not a prosperous business due to her father's illness and his eventual death in 1939.

Helena was one of eight children, four girls and four boys, and she reminisces lovingly about her talented siblings, of whom only three would survive the Holocaust. It was Helena's brother Chaim, a brilliant and rebellious young man, who nourished her passion for reading and learning. Helena attended a prestigious Hebrew *Gymnasium*, whose founder and principal, Dr. Chaim Kugel, was a gifted pedagogue as well as the Jewish Party delegate to the Czechoslovak Parliament. The *Gymnasium* also became the hotbed of Zionist activity in the town.

Before the war, gender roles were carefully prescribed, even in less conservative Eastern European households, with women expected to care for the family and attend to domestic affairs. Helena's passionate desire to get the best possible high school education and then continue on to university flew in the face of tradition. In 1940, she was admitted to the Teachers Training Institute, about a hundred kilometres away from home, where she could pursue her dream of becoming a teacher. Against all odds, Helena became a certified teacher in 1943, which was a decisive experience in her life. Shortly after graduation, she got her first teaching position in a Jewish elementary school in Užhorod, about twenty kilometres away from Mukačevo, where Hungarian was the language of instruction. In the spring of 1944, however, just as she was beginning her new life as a teacher, German troops marched into town. Until then, unlike in neighbouring Poland where the Germans had already massacred millions of Jews, Subcarpathian Jews remained relatively sheltered under the Hungarian occupation despite numerous anti-Jewish laws and restrictions. On March 18, the first day of Passover, all of Užhorod's Jews were rounded up and forcibly relocated to a makeshift ghetto in an old brick factory on the outskirts of town. The living conditions were miserable due to overcrowding, hunger and the lack of sanitation. The majority of the ghetto's inhabitants were transported to Auschwitz and murdered. In a rapid succession of events, Jewish life in the region was swept away.

At the time of the German invasion, Helena considered herself to be a "mother" to an entire group of children, her elementary school students. Her fierce loyalty to them, her belief that she must "support them spiritually and encourage them," did not allow her to go into hiding and save herself. Today, we know the story of Janusz Korczak, the legendary pedagogue and director of the Jewish orphanage in the Warsaw ghetto, who chose to accompany the children in his care to the death camp in Treblinka, despite numerous offers from his friends to help him escape and go into hiding. Like Korczak, Helena also felt that she could not let "her" children down, and her story brings some measure of recognition to the countless teachers and caretakers who must not remain nameless. In the squalor of the brick factory ghetto, Helena continued to take care of her young students, taking comfort in the fact that, despite the hunger and cold, at least they were all together. The worst, however, was yet to come: a few weeks later, all the Jews of Užhorod were crammed into cattle cars and dispatched on a "journey to hell." On the ramp at Auschwitz, Helena caught the last glimpse of her children, most of whom were led straight to the gas chamber. This was also the last time Helena saw her own mother, her "truly exceptional … tolerant and beautiful" mother.

> As Charlotte Delbo, a French survivor of Auschwitz, wrote,
> My mother
> She was hands, a face
> They made our mothers strip in front of us
> Here mothers are no longer mothers to their children.[4]

Under Hitler's dictatorship, the Nazis not only annihilated millions of European Jews and the Jewish presence in Eastern Europe,

---

4 Charlotte Delbo, *Auschwitz and After*, translated by Rosette C. Lamont (New Haven: Yale University Press, 1995), 12.

but they also tried to destroy some of humanity's most fundamental ideals and beliefs, such as the belief that mothers are sacred and deserve respect. On the pages of her memoir, Helena mourns her mother, her wise and big-hearted mother who, before the war, managed to clothe and feed all of her children and even took in an orphan girl from the neighbourhood. She had enough love for all of them, and that love bore the scent of fresh challah that she would bake for Shabbat. In writing her memoir, Helena passes on the *bracha* (blessing) her mother used to recite as she was lighting the Shabbat candles, as if restoring the sanctity of her mother's calling against the degradation of motherhood in Auschwitz. Henryk Grynberg, who, as a young boy, survived the Holocaust on the "Aryan side" solely because of his mother's fierce love and courage, marvels, "How did she manage? Because she was a mother.... Why is it that neither civilians nor the military take this force into account in their plans? This force of mothers."[5] The memory of "her" children is also carved in Helena's heart: tomboyish Judith, artistic Donath, beautiful Eva.... Today, she honours them by sharing her memories with thousands of young people in Canada, in classrooms, at school assemblies, and now in this book.

In 1997, I attended a Yom HaShoah commemoration in Halifax, Nova Scotia and this is where I first heard Helena Jockel's harrowing story: in halting words, she described the Nazi murderers, whom she saw as the epitome of evil that defied comprehension. She spoke of the inferno of Auschwitz in which the most fundamental values that define us as human beings ceased to exist. Yet, to conclude her powerful presentation, she read the following quote from *The Diary of Anne Frank*: "In spite of everything I still believe that people are really

---

5   Henryk Grynberg, *The Jewish War* and *The Victory* (Evanston, Illinois: Northwestern University Press, 2001), 33.

good at heart. I simply can't build up my hopes on a foundation consisting of confusion, misery, and death."[6] When I first invited Helena to speak about her experiences to my students at the University of King's College, she closed her moving exposé with the same quote. In Helena's reading, this expression of belief in the fundamental goodness of men and women does not alleviate the disastrous, traumatizing impact of learning about such horrors; there is nothing redemptive in her story. Instead, she offers a powerful lesson about who we are, who we should be and who we should want to become if we are to call ourselves "human."

In the book you have before you, Helena tries to fathom the SS camp guards' capacity for evil and the "coldness and arrogance" of Nazi bureaucrats such as Adolf Eichmann (whom she once saw with her own eyes), but she prefers to dwell on those who helped her, even if that assistance meant diminishing their own chances of survival.[7] Her memoir conveys to us that even in the most degrading circumstances, in the *anus mundi* of Auschwitz, it was still possible to remain human and not lose faith in human values and ideals. If kindness was possible there, it should certainly be possible here, and this is the belief she wants to instill in the children and youth she teaches today. A telling moment in Helena's memoir that expresses this faith is an episode in which the concentration camp number was tattooed on her forearm. Many survivors speak of the humiliation of being branded like cattle and reduced to a number that erased their identity and their proper names. Amazingly, Helena writes that she was "elated" to get the number because it was unique; there was only one A 16501 (indeed, after the war, her brother was able to locate her

---

6 Anne Frank, *The Diary of a Young Girl* (New York: Bantam Books, 1993).

7 In 1944, Hungary and the entire region formerly under Hungarian occupation came under Eichmann's direct orders.

because of her concentration camp number). In Helena's memoir, the insignia of shame becomes transformed into a reminder of her humanity and, with time, even into a badge of honour.

The desire to recover human values from the cesspool of Auschwitz is also apparent in Helena's evocative descriptions of camp life. She conveys a suffocating feeling of being trapped within the enclosure of electrified barbed wire and of being under constant surveillance, with severe punishments meted out for the smallest infractions. The absolute lack of privacy wore the prisoners down, and Helena writes that "We were never, ever alone." In the barracks, Helena had to share a wooden pallet that served as a bed with fourteen other women, and there were no facilities to maintain even basic hygiene. It was humiliating to not be able to attend to one's basic physiological needs in private. But in the course of Helena's account, the phrase "We were never, ever alone" begins to ring with an altogether different meaning: against the chilling motto "Each man for himself," which, as other survivors often tell us, was the main survival strategy in Auschwitz, Helena never felt desperately lonely and left to her own devices.[8] Even in Auschwitz, there were friends, mostly other women, who came to her aid. There was Terka, a Muslim prisoner, who once helped her clean a soiled latrine and protected her from being beaten, or Regina, a young Polish prisoner who worked as a messenger between the SS officers in the camp and got Helena a coveted job in the kitchen, which most likely saved her life. The advantages of having a roof over one's head and a bit more to eat were immeasurable, as

---

8   In *Night*, Elie Wiesel recalls his father telling him, "Listen to me, kid. Don't forget that you are in a concentration camp. In this place, it is every man for himself, and you cannot think of others. Not even your father. In this place, there is no such thing as father, brother, friend. Each of us lives and dies alone. Let me give you good advice: stop giving your ration of bread and soup to your old father. You cannot help him anymore." Elie Wiesel, *Night*, translated by Marion Wiesel (New York: Hill and Wang, 2006), 110.

was the opportunity to wash herself, which restored to her not only a modicum of hygiene but also a sense of human dignity. Helena tried to return Regina's favour by acting as an interpreter between her and her Czech boyfriend.

Italian Holocaust survivor Primo Levi writes that, in Auschwitz, the inability to communicate – to understand the orders and to obtain life-saving information from other inmates – was deadlier than hunger or physical coercion: "The greater part of the prisoners who did not understand German – that is, almost all of the Italians – died during the first ten to fifteen days after their arrival: at first glance, from hunger, cold, fatigue, and disease; but after a more attentive examination, due to insufficient information."[9] Against the annihilating force of the collapse of language in the camp, Helena used her multilingual skills to connect with others and even to obtain the news of the outside world, which was "like gold." At the time when everything was taken away from her, Helena's most precious possession was her ability to communicate with other inmates in Czech, Russian, German or Hungarian, to use language, that unique human attribute that the Nazis tried to strip away from her. Language made it possible for Helena to discover a community even in the place where it was most difficult to find one: in the *univers concentrationnaire* of Auschwitz-Birkenau.[10] She writes, "There was some comfort in being with the same group of women every day. It made me feel, somehow, more alive."

What emerges from Helena's account is that courage, even heroism, among the women prisoners in Auschwitz meant something altogether different than what we usually take these words to signify.

---

9 Primo Levi, *The Drowned and the Saved*, translated by Raymond Rosenthal (New York: Vintage Books, 1988), 93.

10 The term *l'univers concentrationnaire* to describe Nazi concentration camps was introduced by French survivor of the camps David Rousset, in his 1946 memoir of this title.

Instead, courage meant the will to combat the feelings of worth-
lessness and powerlessness, and to do so with the small gestures of
solidarity, kindness and compassion. There were many precious moments of camaraderie among the women, such as sharing recipes
(cooking with their mouths[11]) and especially singing songs together,
regardless of their poor musical abilities, as Helena adds with a touch
of humour. The value of these moments of togetherness, which "lifted
their spirits" and, for Helena, trumped the evil of the camps, is pow-
erfully conveyed in the title of her memoir: *We Sang in Hushed Voices*.

Another factor that sustained Helena's will to survive was her love
of beauty and her ability to notice it even in the darkest of places.
We rarely read an ode to beauty in an Auschwitz memoir, yet Helena
managed to find beauty even in the midst of horror. One example
is her description of the astonishingly beautiful, "magnificent and
pure" faces of Italian women who arrived one day on a transport.
For Helena, these rare moments of aesthetic rapture had the power
to quell the ugliness around her, to stave off the squalor, and keep at
bay the menace of the SS guards' hateful faces. On the other hand, she
also recalls how unbearable it was for her to witness the degradation
of beauty in Auschwitz, such as hearing Johann Strauss's resplendent
waltzes being played by a camp orchestra composed of inmates who
were once well-known musicians, but who were now being forced to
play for the amusement of the SS. Like her openness and willingness
to share with others, Helena's love of beauty was an indestructible
gift she had received from her mother, who still lives so vividly in

---

11 Holocaust scholar Myrna Goldenberg notes that sharing recipes among female
prisoners was a frequent occurrence in the Nazi camps, and she suggests that it
should be viewed as a uniquely female form of resistance. See Myrna Goldenberg,
"Food Talk: Gendered Responses to Hunger in Concentration Camps," in *Experience and Expression: Women, the Nazis, and the Holocaust* (edited by Elizabeth
Bauer and Myrna Goldenberg, Detroit: Wayne State University Press, 2003),
161-179.

her memory. Today, like her mother in the days of Jewish Mukačevo, Helena likes to be smartly dressed and, as if to remind her of her mother, there is always something beautiful on the coffee table: a bouquet of roses in a flower vase, a pretty china cup, a little lace doily.

On January 18, 1945, Helena left Auschwitz with a column of prisoners and set off on a death march that led her through a series of camps in Germany. It was a nightmarish voyage of which she retains fragmented memories of unbearable cold, exhaustion and death, with only her great will to survive and the need to take care of her sister pushing her onward. And then the nightmare ended. Each Holocaust survivor seems to distinctly remember the moment when he or she realized that the torture was over, and Helena has the most "beautiful and rare" memory of a group of women who celebrated freedom by joining in the singing of the Jewish prayer *Shema*, which refers to the faith and loyalty to one God that is the essence of Judaism.

The women's ordeal, however, was far from over: there was no safety to be found in war-torn Europe. In one of the most chilling episodes, Helena describes the sacrifice of two older Hungarian women who hid her and her sister Agi, but who were themselves brutally raped by Russian soldiers, members of the Soviet liberating army. As Holocaust scholar Myrna Goldenberg has written, we must recognize that although "the hell was the same" for all the victims of the Holocaust, "the tortures were different" for men and women, and it was women who bore the brunt of the additional horror of sexual violence.[12]

Overcoming many adversities, Helena returned to Czechoslovakia and found shelter with her surviving brother-in-law in the town of Znojmo. Bit by bit, she managed to rebuild her life, sustained by her

----

12 See Myrna Goldenberg, "Sex-based Violence and the Politics of Survival," in *Different Horrors, Same Hell* (edited by Myrna Goldenberg and Amy Shapiro, Seattle: University of Washington Press, 2013).

desire to return to teaching as well as by the kindness and understanding of her new friends. She obtained a position teaching English and Russian literature in a high school in Znojmo (although now Czech was the language of instruction), and at the same time began her studies at the university level. She married Emil Jockel, her former brother-in-law, and had two children. We can say that Helena's love of life, which had helped her endure the worst, was finally reciprocated despite the hardships of living in the country that, after the war, became a satellite of the Soviet empire.

Helena came to Canada from Czechoslovakia in 1988 to be with her children and grandchildren, who had emigrated there before her. She left behind her house, her friends, and the everyday comfort of being able to small-talk and joke in one of her native tongues. Helena made new friends in Halifax, joined a book club, and perfected her English. She embraced Jewish spirituality and customs by becoming a member of the Shaar Shalom congregation and she takes special pride in being Jewish, especially because it was denied to her twice before, by two consecutive totalitarian regimes. Without hesitation, she now calls Halifax her home. Yet the Canadian shores were not always welcoming to the Jews, certainly not to those who, in the late 1930s and early 1940s, were trying to escape Nazi murderous policies.[13] The Halifax connection to the story of the fated voyage of the MS *St. Louis* is particularly instructive,[14] as are the stories of Holocaust survivors who, when they first came here after the war, met with indifference, even hostility.[15] In 2011, a memorial monument, called the *Wheel of*

---

13 See Irving Abella and Harold Troper, *None Is Too Many: Canada and the Jews of Europe 1933–1948* (Toronto: University of Toronto Press, 2012).

14 See Sarah A. Ogilvie and Scott Miller, *Refuge Denied: The St. Louis Passengers and the Holocaust* (Madison: WI: University of Wisconsin Press, 2006).

15 See, for instance, Holocaust survivor Israel Unger's account of his family's immigrating into Canada in 1951. Carolyn Gammon and Israel Unger, *The Unwritten Diary of Israel Unger* (Waterloo, ON: Wilfrid Laurier University Press, 2013).

Conscience, was unveiled at Pier 21, Canada's national immigration museum in Halifax. Designed by famous architect Daniel Libeskind (himself the son of Holocaust survivors from Lodz, Poland), the memorial, in the shape of a polished stainless steel wheel, symbolizes the policies and attitudes that prompted Canada to turn away more than 900 Jewish refugees in July 1939. The four interlocking gears on the wheel bear the words "hatred-racism-xenophobia-antisemitism,"[16] reminding us of how fragile our sense of security and well-being is and how quickly attitudes toward those whom we perceive as strangers – because of their religion, their customs or their foreign accents – can turn into genocidal violence.

If Libeskind's monument serves as a warning, Helena's book is a monument to the human spirit; its purpose is to keep the wheel of conscience turning in all those to whom these words are addressed. It is the classroom where Helena has always been in her element. Perhaps the most valuable lessons that she teaches her students is that one of the most effective ways to open people's hearts and conquer their indifference and lack of concern for others is by *opening a book.* Each time I have visited Helena over the years there were new titles on her living room table: I first heard about Ursula Hegi's *Stones from the River* and Toni Morrison's *Beloved* from Helena. She remembered the names of every character in Fyodor Dostoyevsky's novels and all the strange plots in Franz Kafka's stories. For Helena, the respect for human values and the love of reading go together, and this is the gift that she has always wanted to pass on to "her children." Today she has added another gift: we can now open the pages of Helena's own *We Sang in Hushed Voices.*

Helena felt a moral duty to write, even though dredging up the memories of her traumatic past was excruciating. The horrific images return, sharp and crystal clear – Helena still remembers the pungent

---

16 See http://www.pier21.ca/exhibitions.

smell of smoke billowing from the crematoria in which her loved ones became ash. The gift of bearing witness to the past is priceless, but it is her passion for learning, love of beauty, respect for human values and vigilance against injustice that make her lessons of history enduring. It takes immense courage, a big heart and exceptional wisdom to pass them on. Perhaps holding on to these values is the true meaning of survival.

Dorota Glowacka
University of King's College
2014

NOTE: I would like to thank Tamar Wolofsky for helping me tremendously with research for this Introduction. Tamar's family on her mother's side is from the former Jewish community in Sighet.

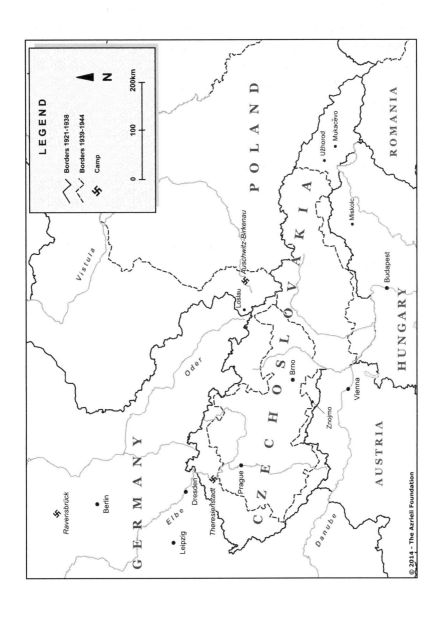

Helena Jockel's Family Tree*

PATERNAL GRANDPARENTS:
Kahan

MATERNAL GRANDPARENTS:
Mendel Berger m. *Zisl Hochman*

AUNT:
Mermelstein

AUNT:
Name Unknown

AUNT:
Taube

AUNT:
Name Unknown

FATHER:
Ben Zion (Bence) m.

MOTHER:
Miriam

BROTHER:
Menusch (Mendu) m. *Hermina* ——————— *Name Unknown*

SISTER:
Jolan (Jolanka) m. *Moszie Fried* ———— *Vera*
Name Unknown

BROTHER:
Jan (Eugene) m. *Monika*

SISTER:
Roszie m. *Emil Jockel* ——————— *Henri*

BROTHER:
Chaim (Kolja)

BROTHER:
Joseph (Jossi) m. *Margaret Emery* ————— *Michael George*
Marie
John
Peter

SISTER:
Agneszka (Agi) m. *Josef Soffer* —— *Ruzena*
Vera

*Helena Kahan m. *Emil Jockel* —— *Jana* —— *Jolana*
born 1919
Pavel m. *Klara* —— *Tom*
Dan

I dedicate these memories to my children, Jana and Pavel, and to all those who suffered such pain, loss and humiliation in the Holocaust.

With this memoir, I celebrate in the name of goodness and beauty, and reject evil in favour of these higher ideals.

To my friend Dorota Glowacka for her personal courage in sharing her knowledge of the Holocaust with her students.

To my friend Carolyn Condé who assisted me with the writing of this memoir.

I did not go back to Mukačevo from Užhorod
to see my brother or my mother.
I felt a loyalty to my students, my "children."
I thought I could help them. We would work somewhere
and support each other spiritually, and I would encourage them
because it was close to the end of the war.
I was not given that chance. The transport arrived at Birkenau,
the smoke was so dark, and I asked, "What is this? What is this?"
The people who worked there said, "Do you have a mother?
Do you have a father? They're burning there."
My "children" too.

Author's Preface

Nearly seventy years have passed since the end of the war and I continue to feel the tragedy of what I lived through, what I witnessed and what I lost. The world's lack of concern – past, present and future – continues to frustrate me. As I write this memoir I struggle with my memories and my pain. I fear my readers will be indifferent to what I went through. And yet, I feel a moral duty toward the people I loved whose lives were so brutally cut short in such a beastly manner, a moral duty to write this – my memoir.

My Mukačevo

Czechoslovakia had only existed as an independent state for one year when I was born; it was only twenty years old when the Nazis occupied it in 1938.

I was born Helena Kahanova on October 23, 1919, in Mukačevo, in Subcarpathian Ruthenia, near the border of Czechoslovakia and Hungary. Czechoslovakia had emerged out of the collapse of the Austro-Hungarian Empire in World War I and Mukačevo is an old city that traded hands between countries and empires multiple times – Mukačevo is its name in Czech, but it has also been known as Munkács in Hungarian, Muncaci in Romanian, Mukaczewo in Polish and Munkatsch in Yiddish and German.[1] Founded in 896, it became part of the Kingdom of Hungary in the eleventh century. Now, one hundred years later, it is called Mukacheve and is part of the Zakarpats'ka province of southwestern Ukraine.

The Jewish community in Mukačevo when I was growing up was large – out of a population of more than 20,000, nearly half were Jewish. There were also a number of schools and political and so-

---

1 For information on the Austro-Hungarian Empire, as well as on other historical, religious and cultural terms; major organizations; significant historical events and people; geographical locations; and foreign-language words and expressions contained in the text, please see the glossary.

cial organizations. Mukačevo attracted cultural troupes from all over Czechoslovakia, too, and there were a wide variety of performances in town.

My roots in Mukačevo went quite far back. My mother, Miriam Berger, was born there, as were my maternal grandparents, Mendel Berger and Zisl (née Hochman) Berger. My grandmother's family had a bakery in the town. My paternal grandparents were from a town called Maramoros Sziget (now Sighetu Marmației in Maramureș, Romania), which was about 130 kilometres away from Mukačevo. My paternal grandmother's name was Chana, but I don't remember my grandfather's name. At some point in the early 1890s, my father, Ben Zion (Bence) Kahan, moved to Mukačevo and married my mother. I was the seventh of their eight children – four boys and four girls – born between 1895 and 1923.

Life for my mother and father was not easy. My father had fought in World War I and had been injured in Italy by a piece of shrapnel. He never fully recovered and was chronically sick with heart problems. Mostly, it was my mother who both worked and raised the children. My mother also took in a girl from the neighbourhood named Shari, whose parents had died. Shari's last name was also Kahan, but she was not related to our family. It was a challenge to clothe and feed all of us – we weren't rich and lived in a small, two-room apartment with a small kitchen and front hall – but my mother was truly exceptional at everything she did. And we all helped each other. By the time I was born, many of my older siblings no longer lived at home, but from the eldest to the youngest, we supported and cared deeply for one another. We were poor, yet we were loved; we had a mother who was tolerant, kind and adored her children.

My parents were Orthodox, although they were not extreme in their practice. My father, who was the more religious of the two, had a small business selling produce from a cart and dressed in civilian clothes, not in traditional Orthodox dress. He didn't have a beard or *peyes* (sidelocks), nor did he wear a traditional black hat. He did, how-

ever, believe in keeping Orthodox Jewish traditions and was very de-
voted to Judaism. My mother kept a strictly kosher home. On Friday
evenings, she laid the table beautifully for Shabbat (Sabbath). She
baked fresh challah bread and made chicken soup with homemade
noodles. Occasionally, my mother, my little sister, Agi (Agneszka),
and I went to synagogue too, but it was not expected that women and
girls attend services. At sundown, my mother lit candles and said the
brachah (blessing) to welcome the Sabbath. I remember the white
lace shawl she wore over her head while reciting the blessing at can-
dle-lighting, and how she always cried when she said the prayer, si-
lently blessing each one of us. Then my father went to the synagogue
for Friday evening prayers. When my father returned from services
he said the *kiddush* blessing over the wine before we sat down to eat
the Sabbath feast.

As we grew older, like many young people, my siblings and I did
not follow my father's Orthodox traditions. Even my mother more
readily embraced modern culture than my father. My father was
someone who had a strong personality and didn't identify at all with
totally assimilated Jews. In his view, Jews who abandoned their faith
and assimilated into secular culture had inferiority complexes – they
were ashamed to be born Jewish. In general, my father was not very
amenable to the outside, non-Jewish world.

My mother, on the other hand, was more liberal and moderate,
more accepting of new things. She was the kind of mother who identified with her children's politics – she wanted to always sympathize
with her children, which my father didn't like very much. She was intelligent, good-hearted and a wonderful role model for her children.
She was attractive, too. I especially remember her lovely hair and blue
eyes. Her legs were like a dancer's, strong and shapely. She also liked
to be fashionably dressed, although she cared more that her children
wore nice clothes. Like me, my mother loved to read; we had a lot of
things in common. My father was not especially good at learning languages, but my mother spoke beautiful German and Hungarian and

was well-read in both languages. She was not only a good role model, she was my everything. To this day, I still mourn her.

My eldest brother, Menusch (Mendu), born in 1893, was a journalist and lived in Užhorod, about forty kilometres northwest of Mukačevo. He married a woman named Hermina and they had a son in 1944.

My sister Jolan (Jolanka), who came next, born in 1902, was a seamstress. She married a Hungarian doctor, Moszie Fried, in 1938 and moved to Nyírbátor, about an hour away by car. They had two children, a daughter named Vera (Verushka), and a younger son, whose name I don't remember.

Jan (Janni or Eugene), third in line, was born in 1905. He volunteered as a soldier in the Czechoslovak Legion and initially fought against the Bolsheviks in Russia; he then became one of 1,500 Czech soldiers who joined the International Brigades to fight against General Francisco Franco's fascist forces in the Spanish Civil War that lasted from 1936 to 1939. He ended up in a prison in France and eventually returned to Mukačevo.

Then came my sister Roszie, born in 1907, who was also a very talented seamstress. She and Jolan would always make new, fashionable dresses for me and Agi. Roszie was especially gifted. If she had lived, she would have probably been a successful fashion designer. She had a small business designing lingerie in Znojmo, Czechoslovakia, a town near the Austrian border in the southern Moravian region. She was so modest and polite in her quiet way. In Znojmo, she married a businessman named Emil Jockel just before the war.

My brother Chaim (Kolja), born in 1913, was an intellectual who spoke all the Eastern European languages as well as French and English – ten languages in total. He studied law and linguistics in Prague and at the Sorbonne in Paris. I believe that Chaim was a genius. As his younger sister, I admired everything about him: his personal courage, his passion and his willingness to fight for his ideals. And the bond was reciprocal; I felt that he trusted and loved me, too.

A committed communist activist, he had moved to the Soviet Union for political reasons. Tragically, this didn't stop him from being executed in Siberia in 1938 – a victim of Stalin's Great Purge.

My brother Joseph, or Jossi as we called him, was three years older than me and also became a soldier. Blond, blue-eyed, and physically very strong, he became an aviation electrician in the exiled Czech Air Force stationed in England. While he was in England he married Margaret Emery, known as Peggy.

My sister Agi, the youngest in the family, was born in 1923. She was very beautiful, and I always felt the need to take care of her.

Like my father, who had fought bravely and was injured in World War I, all four of my older brothers were ready to take up arms and fight. When Hitler declared war, I remember my mother saying, "I gave my husband to the First World War and now I shall have to give my children to this war." In general, my mother tended to sympathize with her children's political points of view. If her children were politically left, so was she. I don't think my father approved.

Like my siblings, I was a high achiever. I loved going to school and was inspired to read and educate myself. Chaim, with whom I had an especially close relationship, was very influential in that regard. On his visits home he would spend time talking with me about ideas and books. My favourite subjects were languages and literature. I didn't have much money, but Chaim and my other siblings brought books home for me. Chaim made a long list of Russian authors and famous titles from German and French literature that he wanted me to read.

I still remember some of the authors on Chaim's reading list: André Gide, Henri Barbusse, Lion Feuchtwanger, Leo Tolstoy, Fyodor Dostoevsky, the highly political Maxim Gorky, and even Vladimir Mayakovsky, a poet of the Russian Revolution. When I was still quite young, Chaim said to me, "You're less beautiful than the other girls in the family, but you're probably smarter. I have a feeling that you'll go to university and study." Perhaps he was joking, but I think he meant it. Chaim was right. I was not as beautiful as my sisters but I did love school.

Before the Nazi occupation, Jewish children in Mukačevo could attend any of the schools in the town. Elementary school began in Grade 1 and continued to Grade 6. We then went to high school, the *Gymnasium*, from ages thirteen to nineteen. There were three high schools in Mukačevo: the Hungarian Commercial Academy, the Czech *Gymnasium* and the Hebrew *Gymnasium*. All three schools gave final matriculation exams upon graduation. I went to the Hebrew *Gymnasium*, which was a large school for the time with about five hundred students, most of whom were Jewish, but not all. A small number of Christian students attended because of its reputation for teaching languages and classics. I had one Catholic classmate, Lenart, who wanted to be a priest. He came to our school because he could learn Hebrew and Latin, neither of which was taught in the other schools. But we had a good grounding in other subjects as well. Because it was state-funded, the language of instruction was Czech and we were taught the regular secondary school curriculum. We also learned English and could choose to learn Russian or French.

I loved learning the Hebrew language and Jewish history. Although the school did not formally teach religion, I was curious about the teachings of the Torah and asked my teachers so many questions. They, of course, were pleased to instruct me and as a result I became quite well-informed about the Hebrew Scriptures. I learned that the Bible is filled with meaningful content and I'm proud to know that it was the basis of Western civilization. There was also a strong emphasis on Zionism and Jewish cultural activity in the school. There were festivals and celebrations, and during Jewish holidays such as Chanukah and Passover, there were musical concerts, plays and dance performances. These were times of potential.

~

I was nineteen years old in 1938 when I graduated from the Hebrew *Gymnasium*. That same year, Germany occupied Czechoslovakia.

To appease Hitler's demands for the Czech Sudetenland – the

borderland areas of Bohemia and Moravia where many ethnic Germans lived – Italy, France and Great Britain signed a pact with him in Munich on September 29, 1938. According to their agreement, Czechoslovakia would give up the Sudetenland and, in return, Germany would remain at peace with its neighbours. That October, Germany occupied the Sudetenland and in November, Czechoslovakia was pressured to cede Subcarpathian Ruthenia and the southern part of Slovakia to Hungary in the Vienna Award. In reality, the Nazi occupation of the Sudetenland was the first step in Hitler's plan to weaken Czechoslovakia and expand the Third Reich.

On March 16, 1939, the Nazis violated the Munich Agreement and occupied the rest of Czechoslovakia, and the provinces of Bohemia and Moravia became a protectorate of the Third Reich. Subcarpathian Ruthenia, where Mukačevo was located, mounted a brief resistance in an effort to establish the independent Republic of Carpatho-Ukraine, but the region was soon invaded by the Hungarian army and was annexed to Hungary on March 23, 1939.

At the time, with Hitler's hatred for the Jews already clear from the news and radio broadcasts, twenty-eight of my classmates left for British Mandate Palestine. Zionism had been a key part of our education at the Hebrew *Gymnasium* and many of the students were involved in Zionist youth movements. Although I wasn't affiliated with any specific Zionist group, just by going to the school I was automatically considered a Zionist. I wanted so badly to go to Palestine with my peers. I supported the idea of a Jewish state and sympathized with the need for a Jewish homeland, but I didn't have the luxury of leaving.

About the time the war broke out in September 1939, my father died of coronary artery disease. The only children left at home were me and my sister Agi. Jolan had met and married Moszie Fried and had moved to Nyírbátor, about one hundred kilometres from Mukačevo, and my sister Roszie had married Emil Jockel in Znojmo. Janni was off fighting fascists and Chaim was in Russia; by then, he had already been killed by Stalin, but we didn't know anything about it yet. Joseph, too, was already out of the house working as an electrician; he would soon join the Czechoslovak Air Force. I had to work to help my mother with money for the household. It was the responsible thing to do.

I spent the next two years teaching in private homes and working as a nanny. I had been a good student and spoke six languages – Czech, Hungarian, German, Russian, Hebrew and English. It was natural for me to earn some money by tutoring and taking care of children in their homes. I enjoyed this work and was glad I could help my mother, but what I really wanted to do was save a bit to go to teacher's college.

Finally, in 1940 I filled out an application to the Teachers Training Institute in Miskolc, Hungary, about two hundred kilometres away. The institute was founded in 1846 and had a reputation as a leader in education. Imagine my excitement when I was accepted! At twenty-one years old, in the fall of 1940, I left Mukačevo for the first time.

As the war raged in Europe, I was busy learning to teach. Roszie and Jolan made me dresses and Jolan, who lived only one hour away, sometimes sent me food. My professional training was of the highest standard and I adored my teachers, whom it was considered polite to address as *néni* (aunt) or *bácsi* (uncle). I remember one teacher in particular, Alice *néni*. She was highly educated and had a single child whom she doted on. I often wonder what happened to her.

The entire experience at the institute had a lasting impact on me both professionally and personally, and in 1943, at twenty-four, I completed my studies as an elementary school teacher. Immediately following graduation, I got a teaching position at a private Jewish elementary school in the city of Užhorod, Hungary. An added bonus was that it was not far from home, only about twenty kilometres away from Mukačevo, in the foothills of the Carpathian Mountains. I was ready to begin my new life.

From Freedom to Slavery

In Užhorod, I rented a room from a woman whom I called Boroš *néni*. I was excited to be starting a job there. Užhorod was a beautiful city with a well-established, large Jewish community that dated back to the sixteenth century. It got its name from the Uzh River, which runs through the centre of the city and divides its old and new sections. At the centre of Užhorod, high up on a hill, was a castle that once served as a fortress, much like the castle in Mukačevo. The castle was surrounded by parkland and the outlying hills where people lived. Like Mukačevo, Užhorod was now part of Hungary and had changed hands many times throughout its history, becoming part of the First Republic of Czechoslovakia when World War I ended in 1918 and the Austro-Hungarian Empire collapsed.

When I lived there, Užhorod had a population of less than 17,000 and out of those roughly 40 per cent were Jews. Many of them were Orthodox who followed the traditional laws and modes of dress, and among the Orthodox were groups of Hasidim led by eminent rabbis. There were synagogues, prayer halls, yeshivas, a Jewish hospital, a Jewish old age home, a Hebrew press and many other Jewish institutions. The central synagogue, built in 1910 and designed in both Byzantine and Moorish styles, was especially beautiful. Since World War II, the original building – prized for both its architecture and its acoustics – has housed the Regional Philharmonic Society and serves as Užhorod's concert hall. Unfortunately, but not surprisingly, all the Jewish symbols have been removed.

The school where I taught, called simply the Jewish School (Židovský Škola), was relatively new; it had been established only three years before, in 1940. The school, housed in a modest, three-storey brick-and-stone building, had five bright, sun-filled class-rooms where five teachers taught a total of forty-five pupils. I still remember a few of the children in perfect detail: Judith Kleinberger, a witty and tomboyish young girl; Donath, a talented, highly imagi-native and artistic boy with beautiful eyes who loved to daydream; and Eva, a beautiful and mature young girl, but so sheltered. Eva was unusually attached to her parents.

When the Nazis occupied Hungary on March 19, 1944, the Jewish School ceased to exist. The Gestapo and SS arrived in Užhorod swiftly and before we knew it, they began to implement anti-Jewish laws. Jewish children were not allowed to go to school anymore. Since there were no classes, my pupils stayed home with their parents. Imagine the contrast – this was a town where Jewish schools of all types had thrived for decades. All of these institutions – elementary schools, high schools, yeshivas, even the Jewish hospital and home for the el-derly – were shut down.

Within a few days, posters appeared around town warning the Jews not to leave their homes in the evenings. On March 31 came the order for all of us to wear yellow Stars of David; these distinctive cloth patches, with a star and "Jew" imprinted on them, had to be sewn onto our clothing by April 5. Without any warning, Jews were also ordered to do so-called community work, which was, in reality, forced labour. We learned very quickly what we had to do – we did what we were told. Otherwise, we all feared that we would be hunted down in our homes and maybe killed.

At first, I was sent to work in the hospital. Since I was a teacher, not a nurse, my job in the hospital was to drag large objects from one floor to the next. My next job was at the Jewish school where I had taught. The Nazis had turned it into an administration centre and the former teachers, including me, had to record information there. That's where I learned that a ghetto was being established and that the Jews were being organized for deportation. We sat at tables while all the Jewish people of the town lined up to report what personal property they owned: houses, furniture, pianos and gold. We had to write down the information and put together reports.

It was there, in my former school, as I sat writing down the details of people's worldly belongings, that I saw Adolf Eichmann. There was a sudden tension in the office and I heard people murmur, "Eichmann is here… he's here." By then I was already familiar with the name and knew that he was high up in the Nazi chain of command – he was in charge of the deportations from Hungary. Only after his trial in Israel in 1961 did it become general public knowledge that he was one of the most horrible killers of World War II, responsible for transporting hundreds of thousands of Jews to the Nazi death camps as part of what was known as the "Final Solution" (*végső megoldás*, we called it in Hungarian), the plan to systematically murder the Jews of Europe.

Even at that time, my impression was that Eichmann was a cold and brutal man. In his crisp uniform and high, shiny boots, he entered the room where I was working with an air of arrogance. He came right up to the table where I was working – there I was, only about one metre away from him. I had a horrible, dreadful feeling when I saw the cruelty in his eyes, a look of willful evil. I could tell that there was not a drop of humanity in this man's heart. He appeared all-powerful, as though nothing could hurt him. I saw one of the elderly gentlemen representing the Jewish community quite literally shaking with fear as he announced Eichmann's visit. The anxiety in the room was palpable. I had no doubt that his aim was to kill all the Jewish people, up to the very last one. This realization shook me to the core.

I had thought of escaping before I was deported; I even had opportunities. One morning, as I was walking toward my former school to work, I saw a group of German soldiers walking down the street. Their uniforms were torn and they looked demoralized. One of the soldiers approached me and said, "You're going to be taken to Poland. Don't go. Come with me. I'll take you to Budapest." I suppose he found me attractive. I was young and good-looking, with long hair. I even remember what I was wearing – a warm beige and brown tweed coat that my mother had bought for me that year for my new job. The soldier and I spoke for about five minutes. I don't know why, but in spite of how short our conversation was, I saw a glimmer of humanity inside of him. It was confusing for me since I knew he was the enemy. This was a significant moment – I could have gone to Budapest with the German soldier. I believe that he would have found a place for me to stay, yet it didn't feel right for me to save my life by running away with the very people who were killing Jews. I wouldn't do it.

I also knew some of my brothers' friends who were not Jewish who could have helped me. If I had gone to their houses, I'm sure they would have hidden me. Everyone knew by then that the war was almost lost for the Germans. What harm would it do for any one of them to hide me? I thought about it seriously. Morally, however, I felt that I could not let "my" children down. All over Europe, the Nazis were killing Jewish children and now my children from the school were about to be rounded up. How could I escape and leave them to their fates? I thought to myself, "No, thank you."

In truth, there were few people who tried to flee the city. We all thought that the war would end very soon. We heard reports every day that Hitler was losing the war and hoped that the Nazi cruelty and racism would end once the Allies won. The situation was very tense; we were all afraid, but we continued to have blind faith in the future.

I felt the desire to live. It was spring, a season of renewal and birth. The sun was starting to shine as we all waited for Pesach, the Passover holiday, to arrive. Passover commemorates the emancipation of the Jewish people from four hundred years of slavery in ancient Egypt.

What terrible irony. Who could have guessed that we were soon to be slaves again? What the Nazis really wanted was to kill the greatest number of innocent Jewish people and children possible, to take away our goods, our clothes, our dresses, everything, by violence.

I was at home alone on one of those chilly spring days when the order came from the Gestapo for us to leave our homes and move to the ghetto. We were kicked out with very little time to prepare. The German officers had sticks and shouted, "*Raus!* Move it! Faster! Move now!" We were only allowed to take a few things with us. I took the clothes I was wearing and my identification. That Passover holiday in April 1944, the entire Jewish population of Užhorod, plus thousands more Jews from the surrounding area, were rounded up and taken to a ghetto in an old brick factory outside of town. Old people, young people, women in the hospital delivering babies, newborns – each and every one of us was thrown out into the street.

Representatives of the Jewish community were placed in charge of the noisy and tumultuous ghetto and were made responsible for getting people ready for deportation. For the next couple of weeks, we slept out in the cold with little shelter. I had only one dress and my spring coat. I was freezing. I stayed with my students and their parents, looking after the children, playing with them and teaching them, while their parents tried to figure out what would happen to us. We only had with us the food we had taken from our homes, which we shared. We thought, at worst, we'll be hungry but at least we'll be together.

Still, we suffered. The anxiety alone was enough to make your heart stop. Waiting out the days, hours and minutes before deportation was sheer torment. It was especially heart-wrenching to see the young children undergo the hardships of hunger and cold, as well as the fear of seeing their parents lose hope. What we experienced then was cruel but none of us could imagine, or comprehend, what was awaiting us. Nobody could. Nobody.

Auschwitz: A Journey to Hell

A few weeks after we had been forced into the brickworks, the Jews in the Užhorod ghetto were stuffed into freight cars and transported to Poland. The guards crammed as many of us as they could into each car – like animals or, perhaps, worse. If horses had been transported in the same type of container, only twelve of them would have fit into each car. In that same space, the Germans packed in two hundred Hungarian deportees. We were deprived of the most minimal human needs: we couldn't stretch; we couldn't wash or use a bathroom; we couldn't take a sip of nice cold water. Nothing was allowed. Nothing.

For three or four days we endured this journey to hell. Without food or water, people began to die. At some point, they stopped the train to throw off some of the dead bodies. The agony was indescribable. I felt desperate. When the train finally stopped and we arrived at Auschwitz, I realized that until then I had no clue what hell really was. Hell is beyond human understanding.

Bright lights shone directly into our faces as we stepped off the train. The harsh glare of the light, after being in the dark for so many days, hurt my eyes. As soon as the doors of the train cars were opened, everything became pandemonium. Barking dogs, trained to attack, snarled and jumped at us. My first thought as I exited the train car was: We are going to die here. I saw smoke. Very thick, black smoke. When I was still in Užhorod, the young German soldier had tried to warn me not to get deported to Poland, but I didn't believe him. I had even heard rumours about gas chambers and crematoria, but I didn't think it was possible. Until that very moment, I had thought that wherever we ended up, I would be able to take care of my children from the school. I would work somewhere... I would shelter them... I wouldn't let them be hurt. Instead, we were all heading to our deaths.

We were ordered to move quickly and stand in a line with other women and children. We were all crying. We had to pass by a row of armed female SS guards who appeared brutal and ugly in their grey uniforms as they looked upon us with hatred. At the head of the line was a good-looking man, standing on a platform, with a few helpers. He was one of the camp's Nazi doctors – it could have been the Angel of Death himself, Josef Mengele. By profession, Mengele was a doctor who worked as a medical officer at Auschwitz. In reality, this man, who had sworn the Hippocratic oath, performed the most abominable medical experiments on women and children – especially on twins. He was obsessed with twins.

When a person reached the head of the line and got to where the medical officer was standing, he pointed either left or right with his fingers. I didn't know this at the time, but to the left were the gas chambers and crematoria – to certain death – while to the right was the camp for forced labourers. I went to the right, assigned to Auschwitz II, also known as Auschwitz-Birkenau, along with the other able-bodied young women. All of the children were taken from us.

Old people, small children and some of the mothers who wouldn't leave their young ones went to the crematoria, thinking they were being taken to the showers to get clean. The mothers went into the showers naked with their children, as did the older people, and they were all gassed. With the SS guards behind us, the rest of us were marched from Auschwitz I to Auschwitz-Birkenau.

It was late morning. Despite our exhaustion and starvation after four days on the train, the SS guards forced us to run. In the group next to mine, I saw a girl from Transylvania who had been a fellow student at teacher's college. She was a pianist, her sister was a wonderful violinist and her mother was an artist. She called out to me by my nickname, Ibi. As she watched her sister and weak, emaciated mother quickly lose strength as they struggled to make it to Auschwitz-Birkenau, she said to me, "You know, Ibi, when I think about taking revenge for this alone – for having to watch my mother and sister dying in front of me – I feel that I would rather go mad." I knew what she meant. The crime that was being perpetrated against her family felt so enormous that it would not even be possible to take revenge. Vengeance, after all, is an endless cycle that only breeds more vengeance and more hatred.

When we finally got to the entrance to Birkenau, we were surrounded by what seemed like endless rows of gates and fences. It was very scary. It struck me as inconceivable, at that moment, that we might be saved or that we were even worth saving. The SS took away our clothes and gave us old, torn dresses. I got a pair of wooden clogs and a worn-out multi-coloured cotton dress. There was a big red X on the back of my dress. I can still see it in my mind's eye. When I asked, "Why is there a red cross on my dress?" I was told, "To make it easier to shoot you if you run away." It wasn't a joke.

We were watched twenty-four hours a day, and the fences, topped with barbed wire, were electrified. Not that it would have been possible to escape. We were never, ever left alone. Inside the camp we were constantly watched by SS guards and by the *Lagerälteste* (camp elder), a fellow prisoner appointed by the SS command to keep us in line and decide what punishments we would receive. Outside were the SS guards with machine guns and attack dogs. On top of all that, there were watchtowers all around the perimeter from which the entire camp and surrounding area could be observed. Not for a minute was there any privacy. Ever.

Two Hours

I was told that in two hours they could kill two thousand people.

Each day, I learned more about the horrors that surrounded me. How could it be that in the twentieth century, mothers and children were burned almost alive? My mother, my wonderful mother, was killed in a crematorium right after she arrived at the camp. People who knew me told me about it. In the camp, you saw the black, black smoke. The people who worked near the crematoria would tell you in a cold and calculating way, "If you have a mother, a father, a brother, a sister, they are here. This is the smoke and the blood of our people."

These were things that I learned on my first day. Jewish prisoners who worked in the crematoria were called *Sonderkommando* (special detail). Every four months the workers were changed and the previous ones were killed. They did this work even though they knew they would die, but in the meantime, they were given better clothing and food, and might even be able to help someone run away. At least, that was the fantasy – that they might be responsible for helping to save one life or perhaps they themselves would miraculously survive. This is what I learned when I asked about the thick, black smoke.

It smelled like burning human flesh. It still makes my skin crawl to think about it. That smell was everywhere, all the time, day and night. You couldn't get rid of that smell. It was all over my body, it seeped into my eyes, my nose, my ears. The smell was always there.

In two hours, they could kill two thousand people.

It was on my second day that I learned about the "special" treatment reserved for women and children. That they were given towels and told to go into the showers to wash. But instead of water, the shower heads contained gas, which suffocated them – suffocated children in the arms of their mothers. Once dead, they were burned in the nearby crematoria. The children, the mothers, the others… in the real sense of the word, they were suffocated, strangled, not able to breathe. Since it was already near the end of the war, it was even worse. The camp was running out of gas, so they had to be stingy and ration the amount used in the showers. The process of dying lasted longer. So the babies died first. Then the mothers who cradled them in their arms. Then the burning of dead people started.

In two hours they could kill two thousand people.

I was assigned to Lager C, Barracks 10, in Auschwitz-Birkenau, along with about eight hundred or a thousand other women. It was an ugly place. In the barracks, there was nothing but a mud floor, a roof and wooden pallets that served as our beds. The roof leaked, so when it rained the barracks floor became muddy. Fifteen women slept on each slab of wood that had nothing but a bit of straw on top. No pillows. No blankets. We could only lie on one side because if you turned over, all fifteen women had to turn at the same time. We turned anyways. There were no toilets, only holes in the ground. There were no showers or sinks, so most people were unable to wash. There were bugs everywhere – all over the barracks and all the places where we worked. There were bedbugs where we slept. And rats. People died of disease from the unsanitary conditions all the time.

In two hours....

Survival

It was my incredible luck that shortly after I arrived in Auschwitz-Birkenau, I met a young woman named Regina and we became very close friends. Regina, who was Polish, had been only thirteen years old when she arrived at the camp. It was extremely rare for a girl so young to survive beyond the initial selection; most went straight to the gas chamber. By the time I met her, Regina was probably fifteen or sixteen. In some ways, she was still a child, but an exceptional, unusually smart child. She saw terrible things, even more than I did, yet she had incredible strength and an unusual instinct for survival.

Regina worked as a *Läuferin*, a messenger and interpreter, in Auschwitz-Birkenau. The *Läuferin* played an invaluable role as a liaison between the *Blockführer* (the leader in charge of a prisoner barracks), the *Kommandoführer*, who was the leader of a specific labour detail, the kapos (prisoners who supervised their fellow inmates) and the prisoners. She had to stand next to the SS guardhouse waiting for orders and if SS officers wanted important messages passed to other officers, Regina would run back and forth with the messages. This gave Regina access to key information that most of us prisoners did not have. In many ways, the *Läuferin* had some semblance of power, at least compared to the powerlessness of other prisoners.

Because Regina knew some of the female SS guards personally, she sometimes received special treatment and could ask for favours.

It helped that she was beautiful. She was often helpful to other prisoners and was therefore also somewhat protected by them. To this day, I do not know why she chose to help me, but I do know that Regina was responsible for saving not only my life, but also that of my sister Agi, who had arrived at Auschwitz from Mukačevo about the same time that I did. Regina helped us intentionally by finding us both jobs in the kitchen. There is no doubt that our kitchen work helped me and Agi survive.

For one thing, in the kitchen I had access to a few of the ingredients that were critical to survival in the camps: I had access to water, which was extremely rare, and I also got some warmth from the kitchen fire. I didn't use soap because I believed the stories that the soap in the camp was made from the fat of human flesh; nevertheless, I was able to wash with warm water and a rag every day. I scrubbed my body vigorously so I wouldn't get lice and scabies or any of the other diseases that were killing so many of the prisoners. Most importantly, I could also get a bit more food (if you could call it that) than most, which I could in turn share with some of my friends. Given that we were on a starvation diet, every little morsel made a difference.

Regina not only helped by getting us work in the kitchen. There were numerous other ways in which I owe my survival to her. She read newspapers and informed me about what was going on with the war, information that I passed on to my group. This made me a kind of authority in the barracks. People listened to me. Any news of how the war was going meant so much to me and my friends. The link with the outside world was invaluable to us.

Out of gratitude, I tried to help Regina in return. I translated secret letters between Regina and her boyfriend, Eric, a Czech prisoner who worked as a maintenance man for the SS. Since they both moved around the camp for work they managed to meet and had fallen in love. Theirs was a passionate connection despite the language barrier. Regina didn't speak Czech and Eric didn't know any Polish, but I helped them communicate with one another. Eric had an important role in my life as well. As a skilled worker who fixed things all over the camp, he, too, had good connections and access to newspapers. After updating me on how the Germans were faring in the war, he would sometimes say, "Pass it on to your girls." When I spread the news in the barracks, knowing that the Germans were being defeated gave us hope. And hope, in Auschwitz-Birkenau, was like gold. Sadly, when the camp was evacuated, I lost contact with Regina. Someone told me that both she and Eric had survived, but that somehow they were lost to each other.

~

The everyday routine of a kitchen worker at Auschwitz was gruelling. Every morning, I was woken up at 4:30 a.m. to go to the kitchen and light the fire under the soup kettles so we could prepare the daily "soup." It wasn't really soup – it consisted of water with a few carrots and rutabagas thrown in. The soup also included a powder called "ava" or "awa" that the kitchen staff scooped out of a paper bag. We were told that the powder was supposed to calm us down so that we wouldn't get overly excited and riot or revolt. We were sure that it wasn't good for us, this ava, but we ate the soup anyway. It tasted bad but gave us some feeling of fullness.

After we prepared the soup, we had to line up in the *Appellplatz*, the outdoor roll-call area. We stood out in the *Appellplatz* at attention until about 7:00 a.m., no matter what the weather was like. We were forced to wait until we were all counted. Then, my group went back to the kitchen to work until noon. Each day at noon all the women stood in line to be given the ersatz soup that we had made in the morning. Thin and watery, it tasted terrible, but at least for an hour or two we didn't experience a feeling of starvation. Then we went back to work until three or four in the afternoon. The other girls who worked with me in the kitchen had the same routine. There was some comfort in being with the same group of women every day. It made me feel, somehow, more alive.

At seven o'clock each evening we lined up outside, at attention, for another roll call in the *Appellplatz*. Standing there, exhausted from hunger and hard labour, we were counted to make sure we were all present. Often, the SS women were not successful at reaching the same number of prisoners as they had counted in the morning. But the numbers were never the same from one *Appell* to the next – how could they be? The dimwitted SS guards didn't even realize that women had died between the morning roll call and the evening one. Nevertheless, when the prisoner count was short, we stood, waiting, until it was corrected. We stood and stood and stood. It could be all night.

In the evening, we were each given a piece of bread that tasted like mud. It was mouldy. Sometimes there was also a piece of hard cheese that came with it. There were times when I would hoard my piece of black, mouldy bread, saving it for later. When I lay down to sleep at night, I put it under my head so no one could steal it. I also slept with my soup cup next to my body to keep it safe. One time, I woke up and realized that the pathetic piece of bread that I had so carefully saved was gone. I cried so hard. Under the circumstances, it was not unreasonable that a fellow prisoner would steal my bread. We all had to survive. But I still cried pitifully for that mouldy bit of bread.

A few weeks after I began work in the kitchen, I got a number tattooed on my arm. Not everyone in Auschwitz-Birkenau received a tattooed number, but the kitchen workers did. You cannot imagine how elated and happy I was when I got that number. It may seem strange that getting a number was something positive for me – most of us believe that being identified solely by a number is humiliating and degrading. In this case, however, I imagined that somewhere, somehow, the truth would come out. To me, that number on my arm meant that I was unique and identifiable – and that I could be found by someone. In fact, in the end, it was because of that number, #A16501, that my brother Joseph was able to find me in Prague, after the war.

～

It hardly seems possible that amidst the horror and the chaos at Auschwitz-Birkenau, I could have recollections of some experiences of astonishing beauty and great poignancy. And yet, I do. One of those instances involved a group of Italian women who arrived just a few weeks after I did. They were artists, or more specifically, engravers. I don't remember how I found out this detail, but somehow I knew their profession. What I remember most is that these women were hauntingly beautiful. They had sorrowful eyes, full of pity and regret.

The Italian women stuck together as a group. It felt like such a tragedy that nobody could speak with them. I think they spoke Italkian, a Judeo-Italian dialect. Since I knew Latin and a bit of Hebrew from school, I was able to have a bit of an exchange with them, with the help of some hand gestures. What impressed me was that in order to survive they seemed to be blocking out the tragic reality in which they found themselves. I tried to convey to them that what they were experiencing was not normal. I tried to tell them that we loved them. To me, these women were spiritually and physically magnificent. They appeared to be so pure, so naïve, their hearts open with an emotional transparency that penetrated my soul. I still do not clearly understand why my encounter with them had such a powerful and lasting effect on me. I was strangely affected by them, even to this day. None of them survived. Not one.

That spring, around the same time that I met the Italian women, I spotted my eldest sister, Roszie, through the electrified barbed-wire fence that separated various sections of the camp. She was holding her infant son in her arms. I had lost touch with her when she and her husband, Emil Jockel, had been deported from Znojmo in 1941 and I didn't even know that they had a child. They had been sent to the Terezin (Theresienstadt) concentration camp in 1942, where she had given birth to their son, Henri, in 1944.

Some months later, all three were moved to the Czech Family Camp in Auschwitz-Birkenau, known as the *Familienlager Theresienstadt* (Theresienstadt Family Camp). The men, women and children in the so-called family camp were assigned to separate barracks, but they were allowed to gather together in the open space outside their barracks. When I saw Roszie, it was from a distance of about twenty metres. All we could do was shout at each other over the fence dividing the sections of the camp. We weren't close enough to have a proper conversation. We spoke like this a few times over the next days and I was able to learn about what had happened to her since we had last seen each other. One of the things Roszie told me stuck with me: if she died and I survived, she told me, she wanted me to take care of her husband and little Henri.

From mutual acquaintances, I was able to figure out what happened to Roszie next. The *Familienlager* was scheduled to be liquidated in July 1944. Out of 11,000 prisoners held there (from the original transports of 20,000), those who were young and healthy were selected to work in other concentration camps. Roszie was among them. She told me that she planned to give her baby a sleeping pill so that she could sneak him out with her, but sadly, the baby woke up and the SS guards took him away from her before she left.

An aunt of ours was also in the family camp with Roszie. Because she was old, she was not selected to leave Auschwitz-Birkenau and little Henri ended up with her. So they stayed in the camp, my aunt and little Henri. Then, from July 10 to July 12, 1944, with dogs and sticks they came. The SS took the old people and the young children, about seven thousand people, including my aunt and my nephew Henri, to the gas chambers. I heard the barking and the screaming. The liquidation of the family camp was complete.

⁓

In addition to these individual tragedies, every day at Auschwitz held a new humiliation. We were not allowed to speak to the female SS guards directly. We had to wait to be addressed and then follow orders absolutely. One time, someone in the camp had broken one of the tanks in the latrine. There was human waste on the floor and the smell was disgusting. An SS woman ordered me to clean it up and as I started to clean the latrine, I began to gag and wanted to vomit. The guard kicked me with her high boots and beat me. Another prisoner, Terka, a Muslim girl, saw what was happening and jumped in to help me. She cleaned the latrine with me while covering me with her body so I didn't get killed. I felt so humiliated and ashamed. I suffered not only from the pain of the beating, but also from an overwhelming feeling of helplessness. It was difficult to accept that one human being could inflict that much misery and torment on another.

I often felt worthless. It was clear to me that our lives were not worth anything. In the kitchen one day, a female SS guard said that she was surprised that Agi was Jewish since she was so attractive. The guard had been taught that Jewish women were covered in hair and crawled on all fours when no one was looking. In the eyes of the SS, we were worse than animals because we were worthless. Worthless as Jews, worthless as women, worthless as human beings. When a human life is not appreciated there is nothing much you can do to protect yourself or others. You have no power. You cannot explain your actions or defend yourself. You are totally exposed and totally vulnerable.

The small acts of courage were what made it possible to survive. One evening, for example, we were made to stand for hours and hours in the *Appellplatz* for roll call. When we were finally released, some of the women who needed to go to the bathroom went straight to the barracks to relieve themselves in the latrines. When they got there, however, the doors were locked. A few of the poor women were truly in agony after holding it in for so long. Not being allowed to empty their bladders was torturous. This was the last straw for some of us, and we began to shout in resistance, "Let us pee!" over and over again. "Don't let them suffer!" I called out. "Don't torture people so much!" One of the female SS guards heard us yelling and came to the barracks.

The guard must have recognized my voice because she came directly over to me, as if I were to blame for the rebellion. The other women were sure that I would be killed. Then, something unexpected happened. A friend of mine from Mukačevo, a woman named Hilda, came to my aid. I had known her before the war, and she was normally very quiet and reserved. Yet, she rallied everyone together and encouraged them all to shout. All seven or eight hundred women in the area began shouting so loudly and with such intensity that the female SS guard grew afraid and left.

There was another way that we could resist – with hope. As we sat on the hard wooden bunks in our barracks, with only our thin, torn dresses to cover us, we still hoped that we would survive. Some of us even tried to learn new languages. By that time, I had already learned some English and spoke it quite well. I also still remembered Hebrew from high school and taught Hebrew words to my friends. It was a time of emptiness, pain and desperation, a time when it was impossible to imagine a way out. There was no way out. But I often thought about miracles.

An extremely important part of our resistance was singing. Although it seems paradoxical to talk about music and Birkenau in the same breath, singing was a key part of our existence. When our work was done and the guards weren't present, we could find safe moments to sing Hebrew songs. We had to be careful never to sing in front of the SS because they would have beaten us to death. I couldn't sing well, but it didn't matter. None of us were really singers. I would teach my friends the words to songs I had learned in school and the women with good voices would figure out the tune. Together we combined words and voices, our voices hushed so that no one would hear us. It gave us encouragement and lifted our spirits; in those moments, we didn't speak about death and killing.

These were not the only music events in the camp. There were also concerts organized by the SS – although these were hardly happy occasions for the Jewish prisoners. I recall one concert that was spontaneously arranged under orders from the camp administration.

We were called out to the *Appellplatz* and commanded to sit on the ground. What we saw in front of us was a group of men in their filthy, striped prison uniforms, emaciated from hunger, each one holding a violin, a cello or a wind instrument. They were told to take their places on a platform and began to play – and, oh, how beautifully they played. Starving and ill, the musicians played waltzes by Johann Strauss II while the SS guards danced to the music.

I began to cry. I cried inconsolably because those musicians were playing music that had been created to make the world a more harmonious and beautiful place. Yet, these men, imprisoned and starving, were forced to play through suffering and humiliation. Strauss's waltzes and operettas, which brought joy to listeners for a hundred years, had nothing in common with Hitler and his ideology.

The Death March

On January 18, 1945, the SS removed us from Auschwitz-Birkenau, from the entire nightmare of a place. Knowing that they were on the verge of defeat, the Nazis tried to wipe out the traces of their inhumane treatment of us, to destroy the proof of their evil deeds and make us, the evidence, disappear. As a result, they dragged us all over the place. They didn't even know where to take us. And so, we wandered, with barely any food. For almost four months, we wandered and wandered and through the wanderings landed in one concentration camp after another. This was what is now known as one of the "death marches."

My memories of the death march are scattered – I cannot recall the sequence of events precisely as they happened simply because it was too traumatic. I can't remember most of the endless days and nights of marching, of starving, of freezing, of trying to take care of my sister Agi, of my own physical pain and tortured mind. The mind blocks out what is too painful. We met Italians, we met slave labourers and French prisoners. I got a picture of the degenerate, perverted aspects of Germany.

From the bits and pieces I do remember, I have figured that first we walked from Auschwitz-Birkenau to the German city of Loslau (now Wodzisław Śląski, Poland) in the western part of Upper Silesia. At that point, we were put into open rail cars and left there all night in the cold. The next day, we travelled nearly six hundred kilometres north to the Ravensbrück women's concentration camp about ninety kilometres north of Berlin, where the inmates included Roma, Jews, political prisoners and children. I'm not sure how long we stayed there. Next, we were marched on a long, torturous route south to Leipzig and then Dresden in the most brutal winter conditions. We arrived in Dresden at the end of April 1945, in the last few days of the war.

This whole period was chaotic. Sometimes I recall episodes of great humanity; sometimes I recall episodes of the greatest inhumanity imaginable. There were times when we travelled in open freight cars, but when Hitler's retreating army passed our convoy, they threw us out of the train cars. We had to walk long distances. It was exhausting and people died. Still, we walked. We slept wherever there was an empty space or place. It could be a warehouse or a barn or just a field.

It was very cold in the first three months of the death march. I was freezing and feeling hopeless. We hardly had any food. I had only a dress and wooden shoes. My shoes were simple and didn't quite fit, but that wasn't the point – I needed to prevent my feet from becoming totally frostbitten. The shoes were my most valuable possession. They were painful but precious in helping me survive.

Sometimes people on the march tried to steal shoes. Not only shoes, but also the little bits of mouldy, dirty, stale food that the SS occasionally handed out. Just as I did in the barracks at Birkenau, I slept with my food and shoes under my body to protect them at night. The people who stole the bread and the shoes were not thieves. They were simply fighting for their lives. I admit that there were times when I was tempted to steal food, but I could never do it. Even in those desperate times, it didn't sit well with my conscience or my ethics to take the single most important thing – that piece of old, stale bread – from the person who had it. Mostly I ate any bread I got right away. I never kept it for long because I was afraid someone would take it and I would die. We barely got two hundred calories a day.

I still don't understand how I survived in the bitter cold. Once when we stopped someplace for the night, Agi and I took off our dresses and washed ourselves in the snow. We wore the same clothes every single day and then slept in them at night. We were sick and hungry and had lice. The only thing that made me put one foot in front of the other was that the guards would have killed me if I didn't. I knew I wanted to survive.

In Leipzig our group stopped and I worked in a munitions factory with some Soviet workers. They were friendly and very nice, very human. They showed me, with gestures, how not to work so hard. I copied what they did to avoid work and somehow conserve energy. It was risky because it was also a kind of protest and if the managers noticed, I would have been killed. I was weak by that point and could hardly work anyway.

After about two straight months on the death march, Agi got sick and her energy was completely drained. She looked like a dying horse – there was so much inexpressible suffering in her eyes – and I thought she might die. When we passed a horse stable, I took the opportunity to drag Agi over to it for a bit of rest and shelter. I was so relieved that she could lie down in the hay for a little while so I could take care of her. But then, the German farmer who owned the stable spotted us. He started telling me in German that we were disturbing the horses, but I didn't respond. I did speak a little German, but I decided to remain silent and pretend not to understand. For some reason, he left us alone. We stayed in that stable for two or three days. Eventually, though, we had to move on. A fellow prisoner found us and helped me with Agi, who was now at least able to drag her feet along a bit. We continued to follow the march.

Three or four days before the war ended, a tragic thing happened to two Lithuanian sisters who were part of our group. They had miraculously survived five long years at Auschwitz-Birkenau and were so close to being free. We were walking past a field where German farmers were planting potatoes near the road and, out of desperation, one of the sisters ran about ten steps away from the group and stole a potato. She was starving and didn't think about what could happen to her. The SS guard who was supervising us shot her. She wasn't even dead yet when he dug a hole in the ground and buried her. Her surviving sister went mad, crying and wailing that she was going to kill the guard. We all surrounded her to protect her from a certain death. It was hard to go on after that, but it was almost the end. We felt it.

On April 30, 1945, Hitler killed himself. I remember the day that I heard about it. I was glad; it meant the war would soon end. Yet there was no jubilation among our group. We were too hungry to celebrate. We began to make pretend meals, sharing recipes. Step by step, we discussed how we would make certain dishes that we loved. We had done this over and over again during the death march. As soon as three women got together, that's what they would do. For some reason, when two women were together no one spoke about food; the imaginary recipes and meals only began when three or more women were together. I begged them not to do it. Anything but that! I was so hungry that I thought I would go mad.

There were about forty of us left in our group when we finally approached the city of Dresden. Everything there had been reduced to rubble when the city was bombed by the Allies in February and some parts were still smoldering from the last bombing a few weeks before. We arrived at night. When we saw the signs of bombing we became hysterical because we were afraid we would be killed. It was so confusing. It was so close to the end – we knew these were the last days of war – yet we were still terrified that the SS was trying to kill us. They would have killed us, too, but they still needed us.

The two SS guards, one male and one female, who had accompanied our group on the march were the most cowardly of all human beings. We were sick, exhausted and helpless; they had guns. Yet, when we got to Dresden, they dressed themselves in civilian clothes and hid among us because, knowing that the Soviet army was so close, they were afraid that they would be killed. Suddenly, they were speaking to us nicely, pleading that what they had done was not their fault. They were innocent, they said, only doing what Hitler told them to do; they were just following orders. As they declared their innocence, we wept. I'm not sure if it was out of relief or because there, in the rubble of Dresden, the evidence of so much destruction and devastation finally sank in.

Amidst the chaos, the noise, the cries, I suddenly heard someone singing Hebrew words. It was Leah, a Slovak-Jewish girl from our group. She was standing up and singing the well-known Jewish prayer, *Shema Yisrael* (Hear, O Israel, the Lord is our God, the Lord is One.) The *Shema* is the Jewish declaration of faith. It is the first prayer that a Jewish child learns and, traditionally, the last words a Jewish person says before he or she dies. Leah had such a soothing voice. Soon, each one of us joined in singing the prayer with her, each in her own language and voice, yet unified by our suffering. It was the single most hopeful moment of my ordeal in the Holocaust. It was also a profoundly soulful, beautiful and rare human moment in that quagmire of inhumanity.

Afterward, we all fell asleep. In the morning, we realized that under cover of darkness the SS guards had disappeared. Cowards. When we were most vulnerable and powerless, naked and exposed, without a hope in the world, they had revelled in our humiliation. They had relied on our defenselessness for their power. Not one of them had the personal courage to help us or even to question what they were doing to us and why.

How could this have happened? Where was humanity? Where were the people with human kindness in their hearts? Why did they not help us? That is what I kept asking throughout my time at Auschwitz-Birkenau and it is what I asked myself on that day at the end of the death march. It is what I am still asking today, almost seventy years later.

Personal courage can mean many things, but first and foremost it entails compassion. Neither the perpetrators of the Nazi crimes against the Jews   nor those who knew what was happening and re-mained silent – showed compassion. Personal courage also means being brave, brave enough to take action when you don't agree with what is going on, so that you make your voice heard. Hitler never made a secret about his desire to kill the Jews. Yet, no one took any real steps to stop the murders. Not the United States, not Britain, not the individuals who stood by and watched.

Some Place Called Home

Germany surrendered unconditionally to the Western Allies on May 7, 1945. By this time, about ten or twelve people were left in our group in Dresden, most of us from Mukačevo and the surrounding area. I was happy to be free. In spite of the suffering and feeling weak from our brutal treatment, I felt happy. I was still young, the trees were in bloom, the sun shone, and we had been miraculously saved.

After the Allied bombing of Dresden, many Germans had fled the city and a great number of houses around us were empty. We went into these houses without any feelings of guilt whatsoever. We washed ourselves, slept and took whatever clothes we could find that fit us. We still must have looked insane. As we walked around Dresden, we saw the Germans staring at us peculiarly. They had apparently been told that we were war criminals who had prevented Hitler and Nazi Germany from ruling the world. It still did not occur to them that Nazi propaganda had fed them lies and hatred. I suppose that many of them still believed the mythology that Hitler was a perfect and wonderful leader. There were, however, some Germans who cried and apologized when they found out about the concentration camps. When I saw them cry, I felt there was still some kindness in the world.

As soon as we were strong enough, some of us from Mukačevo set out for home. But was it still our home? What was home? Walking purposefully but without much direction, Agi and I, along with a few other women, set out on the long journey, heading toward the

Czech border. We periodically found our bearings by asking people we met how to get out of Germany and find our way to Prague. We wandered from place to place, asking directions from both ordinary Germans and *Fremdarbeiter*, foreign workers who had been brought to Germany from other countries as forced labourers, and set our mental compass south toward the border.

We had a variety of unforgettable encounters along the way. One awful experience repeats itself over and over in my mind to this day. While we were still in Germany, but close to the Czech border, Agi and I, plus two other women from our town, found an empty house where we could rest for a day or two. Our two companions were quite a bit older than us, perhaps forty-five or fifty years old. One of them, Rita, I had known vaguely from Mukačevo.

As we settled in for the evening, several Russian soldiers came into the house. By the tone of their voices, I instinctively sensed danger. Agi and I hid under a bed where we could not be seen. From our hiding place we could hear the conversation between the soldiers and the older women. I heard one of the women telling the other in Hungarian, "Don't let the girls be raped. Let's offer ourselves and save the girls." When Rita was attacked, she screamed, "Dai! Dai!" which is the Hebrew word for stop, but sounded like the Russian word for yes. I believe that this tragic double entendre gave permission to the Russian soldier to rape her.

We all screamed, and our cries were heard through the open windows of the house by a higher-ranking Soviet officer, who ordered the two soldiers to leave. I don't know for certain what happened to Rita, but her remarkably selfless act of putting herself in danger to save me and my sister from being raped has stayed with me my entire life. I also thought about the soldiers' actions. I came to believe that although the Soviet army had to do whatever they could to defeat the Germans, war is still a sin against life. I believe that because of what they were trained to do in the circumstances of war, the soldiers lost their sense of morality and humanity toward women.

These were not the only soldiers our little group of survivors encountered on our way home. Soldiers from all over Europe were trying to find their way home in the post-war confusion. On one occasion we met up with a group of Italian soldiers who had been fighting under General Pietro Badoglio. He had been a member of the Italian fascist party led by Benito Mussolini, but after a disastrous few years of war on the side of the Germans, in July 1943, the Italian government had removed Mussolini from his position and named Badoglio prime minister of Italy. General Badoglio's regime dissolved the National Fascist Party and surrendered to the Allies, signing an armistice agreement in September 1943. Italy then declared war on Germany in October.

The Italian soldiers had been fighting against Hitler for over a year, but some animosity toward them remained – especially from the Soviets – because of their pro-Hitler past. Unable to speak German or Russian, they were incapable of explaining themselves. With my bit of Latin, I was able to understand their Italian when they spoke very slowly and I promised to help them. When a high-ranking Soviet officer and his soldiers challenged the Italians, I was able to intervene. I explained to the officer in Russian that these Italian soldiers had fought against Hitler. I told him that we were all "international," meaning that we were not nationalists, nor were we fascists. To my great surprise, the Soviet soldiers let them go.

One of the Italian soldiers, Giuseppe, was especially kind to me. He seemed to be attracted to me, and his friends, the other soldiers, encouraged him to pursue me because they wanted my translation help to continue! I don't know whether he was serious or joking, but Giuseppe asked me to marry him. When I said, "No, I am Jewish," he replied, "Don't worry. We will go to the Pope, he will do this [he made the sign of the cross] and it will all be fine." I told Giuseppe that while I was flattered, he should find an Italian woman to marry and I would marry a Jewish man. That was the last time I saw the Italian soldiers. I'm sure they returned safely to Italy.

Slowly but surely, our small group from Mukačevo made our way to Prague. We had stuck together through the death march and were determined to reach our destination by any means we could. Everything in Germany reminded us of the terrible experience we had endured – the suffering, the ill treatment.... We wanted to get as far away as possible from all of it. We stopped military cars, we took rides on horses and buggies, and we walked. It was beautiful outside, the sun was shining and some people stopped to offer us food and bread. There were also organizations that distributed food to war refugees in a number of the places we passed. We had no money at all and we took advantage of any offer of help that we could.

When we finally arrived in Prague, we found the city filled with compassion. The hospitals and the Red Cross were already prepared for the influx of people needing help. Because of the war, they were short on supplies, but whatever they had they gave us. It was especially encouraging to be treated with such consideration because our hearts were still bleeding. We were devastated that we had lost our families. Agi and I were also terribly weak and needed rest, recovery and food.

~

Knowing that my beloved mother died in the gas chambers of Auschwitz is a horror that I will carry with me forever.

After the war I also learned the fate of my sister Roszie, who had contracted typhus sometime during the war. She had survived the camps, but died from her illness just before liberation. I also heard about my other sister, Jolan, who had been deported to Auschwitz two years before me along with her husband, Moszie Fried, and her two children. Vera was only six when she and her mother were selected for the gas chamber immediately upon their arrival at the camp. I don't know what happened to my little nephew, whose name I have forgotten. Jolan's husband was also killed, but I don't know when.

My eldest brother, Menusch, along with his wife, Hermina, and their infant son had been deported to Auschwitz in 1944. Hermina survived, but Menusch and the child were killed.

When my brother Janni returned to Mukačevo from France, he was deported to Auschwitz, where he was tortured but survived. Traumatized by his suffering, he returned to Mukačevo to discover that his beloved had married someone else while he was gone. He was a broken man. Although he managed a large factory in Mukačevo for the next twenty years, he struggled with alcoholism and depression. He died in hospital in Mukačevo in 1977.

I feel terribly sad when I speak about my dear mother, my siblings and my friends from school. I think about how many others I grew up with in Mukačevo who were among those destroyed by Hitler – talented, intelligent young people who believed in human values and ideals.

~

It turned out that my brother Joseph was in Prague as well, looking for family members. He had survived the war in England as part of the Czechoslovak Air Force and married an English woman named Margaret (Peggy). They had had their first child, Michael George, in England in 1945. Immediately post-war, Joseph, Peggy and George re-located to Prague and moved into an apartment. Miraculously, Joseph found us and it was heartening to see him alive. He invited us to live with him and we stayed two or three weeks. It was a vulnerable time for all of us. My brother gave us what we needed to gain strength, and it felt so good to be with two of the siblings I had left.

Unfortunately, Prague was soon in political turmoil once again. The Communists announced that Czech foreign minister Jan Masaryk, the son of President Tomáš Masaryk, had committed suicide by jumping out of a window. Secretly, everyone believed that it was the work of the Communists, and this continues to be a controversial topic. What is not controversial is that men like Joseph, who had fought in England, were persecuted because they were suspected of being anti-Communist and pro-West. Joseph soon realized that staying in Prague might not be the best option for him and his family, so he, his wife, Peggy, and their little boy, George, went back to England. Over the next years, they had three more children; Marie, born in 1947; John, born in 1950; and Peter, born in 1954.

I too was worried about my future. How would I start over again? When would I be able to live a normal life? These were the kinds of questions that kept running through my mind. When I thought about my murdered pupils I felt desolate. Without my teaching, I had no means of making money and no resources. Everything had been taken from us. I had such aspirations when I set out to become a teacher. Because I was still young and had a life ahead of me, I found in myself the strength to pick up the pieces and begin life once again.

After bidding Joseph and his family goodbye, Agi and I decided to head to Znojmo, where Roszie and Emil had lived before the war. I remembered my bizarre, urgent conversation with Roszie through the electrified wire fence between Birkenau and the Terezin Family Camp. She had wanted me to take care of her family if I survived and she didn't. Roszie's husband, Emil, was still alive and living in Znojmo. There was at least one person with whom we had a connection.

In the last days of the war, Emil had been on a forced march that ended at the Terezin concentration camp. Upon liberation, Emil had returned to Znojmo, where he was able to reclaim his house. He had been a businessman before the war and was able to continue this work, which meant he had some means.

When Agi and I arrived on his doorstep, we were penniless, without a home and without any belongings. We were so dirty that Emil made us wait outside while he got some water and soap to wash our feet. Only then did he allow us to go into the house. Emil ended up being very kind. He allowed us to stay with him and took good care of us until we could figure out how we wanted to live.

My first priority was to heal myself physically. I was able to do that, slowly but surely, because I had a place to stay and because I knew that I would be cared for, at least for awhile. In that sense, my physical healing and adjustment to a new reality was not very complicated. Psychologically, it was far more difficult. I had lost my parents, sisters, brothers and friends. Even the people I knew in Birkenau – those who had survived the camp and the death march with me – had gone their separate ways. Agi and I felt pain in our hearts. Somehow, secretly, I hoped for a miracle – that perhaps somebody who had been lost would suddenly show up. It is hard to imagine the loneliness and bitterness of those of us who survived.

It very quickly became clear to me that if I wanted to make it alone, without much family support, I had to do something with myself – and for myself. The one lucky thing was that I still retained my passion for teaching. Not only did I want to be back in the classroom, but I also wanted to find a way to pass on human values and lessons about the world to my pupils. Finding a way to continue to teach became my next priority.

There were several challenges that I had to meet before I could teach again. First, I had to get certified to teach in Znojmo, where the first language was Czech. My diploma from the Teachers Institute in Miskolc was only for teaching in Hungarian. I therefore had to pass an exam in the Czech language in order for my diploma to be acknowledged. Next, although I was qualified to teach at the elementary school level, I felt that this was not where my strengths as a teacher lay. For the most part, I couldn't sing or draw very well, which are valuable and desirable skills for teaching young children.

What worked to my advantage was that there was a shortage of high school teachers immediately after the war. My training in foreign languages, including Russian and English – and my knowledge of literature, history and culture – also served me well. With that kind of background, I was able to get a teaching position at the *Gymnasium* in Znojmo on the condition that I got my high school teacher's diploma at the same time. As soon as I took the test to qualify teaching in Czech, I was hired to teach Russian and English literature to students from Grades 9 to 12.

I met a teacher at the *Gymnasium*, Slavka Dvoracek, who was perhaps four or five years older than me and had graduated from Masaryk University in Brno in 1938. She was a wonderful person and we became very close friends. She encouraged me to attend Masaryk University and to enroll in the philosophy faculty. Brno was about one hour on the bus from Znojmo and Slavka, quite literally, led me by the hand and took me there by bus and helped me register for classes.

That year, in 1946, my life began to slowly change. I attended university classes one day a week while teaching at the *Gymnasium* the rest of the week. I majored in Russian and English, not only mastering the languages, but also learning about the history, philosophy and politics of these cultures. My studies in the Faculty of Philosophy gave me so much pleasure and, at the same time, I loved teaching at the high school. My colleagues there were wonderful to me and I made many close female friends.

Some of my teacher friends had, like me, gone through the war and become disillusioned with the political situation in Europe. Many found an alternative solution in the communist movement, mainly because the capitalist system had been such a disappointment to them. They condemned the cruelty of the Holocaust – and always in a loud, clear voice, so that I heard their opinions.

One close friend, Slavka Vojachskova, was a staunch communist. Like my other friends, she was an intelligent and good-hearted person who acted out of a sense of justice.

Each one of these friends helped me to heal. They were considerate and showed compassion toward me. They knew that I was vulnerable because of my experiences in the war and they constantly buoyed my confidence by showing me how important I was to them. Through my friendships in this wonderful group of colleagues, I found out what it was to live again with human kindness, free of religious intolerance and discrimination. They helped me to feel worthy again.

While I continued studying and teaching, Agi and I continued to live with our brother-in-law, Emil. She soon met a man, Josef Soffer, and when they married, she moved out of the house. It was then that it became apparent that my relationship with Emil was developing into a deep and enduring friendship. At the end of 1948, I married him. He was a good man, a decent man, and I had a good life. It may not have been a passionate relationship, but perhaps another man would not have allowed me to study and be independent, as Emil did. He admired my ambition, my desire to become a professional and earn my own money. They were not bad qualities on which to base a life with someone. For the rest of our married life, I always felt supported.

Steps Toward a New Life

After being married for one year, I passed my state examinations in English and Russian in 1949, then graduated from Masaryk University with my official diploma as a high school teacher. I had worked hard for the degree and I was proud.

The period from 1949 to 1968 was a good and peaceful time. I had finished my studies and enjoyed my work at the *Gymnasium* in Znojmo. In October 1949, I gave birth to my daughter, Jana. Four years later, in 1953, our son, Pavel, was born. I loved teaching, I loved my students and I always got along well with the class. It was satisfying to know that I could contribute something positive to my students' lives.

Emil also worked hard to provide us with a good life. We had many friends and an active social life. Cultural life in Znojmo was especially vibrant at the time. When theatre groups came from Prague to perform, it was always a wonderful event. I would go to the hairdresser and put on a beautiful dress. Sometimes Emil and I went dancing – Emil was an excellent ballroom dancer and taught both our children to dance.

We had a beautiful home that was originally the house of the first mayor of Znojmo, Mr. Mares. We purchased it together with another family and we lived on the top floor while the other family lived on the main floor. It was a classic urban apartment at the end of a long, climbing roadway on the top of a hill, situated about five hundred metres below Znojmo's original, old beautiful synagogue that was built in 1888 and destroyed by the Germans on Kristallnacht in November 1938.

I loved my house because it was spacious and bright, with lots of windows, and was only a ten-minute walk from the centre of town. We had a sizable kitchen with a small room off of it that at one time had probably been a maid's room. There was one other small room and three large rooms that were open concept. At the front of the house was a garden filled with beautiful red roses and a long set of stairs that marked the beginning of our property. I have always loved roses because I find them so expressive and noble. In our search for beauty, they pull us in, beckoning us to recognize and appreciate their loveliness. In the other part of the garden, toward the back of the house, were at least a hundred fruit trees, chiefly apricot, but also cherry, plum, apple and walnut trees. It was a very big property.

Even though these were good times, I can't say that every part of it was ideal, especially in terms of politics. Joseph and his family had already left because of the political conditions under the Communist regime. I wanted to visit them in England very badly. They lived in Orpington (Kent) and I had never met their three younger children, Marie, John and Peter. I applied to the Czech government eleven times for an exit visa before I was finally granted permission to go with Jana in 1962.

I was also the only Jewish teacher in the whole region, which, under the Communist system, was not that easy to handle. Virtually none of the 675 Jews in Znojmo had returned after the war. Most had been deported to Auschwitz. Even today, the Jewish population in Znojmo is about ten people. I didn't have problems with antisemitism, but there were things that I could not say or express freely. I didn't speak about the politics of the Holocaust and World War II, mainly because I would have had to give students the official Communist line that the capitalists were to blame for everything and the communists had played no part in any of the destruction wrought by the war. I wouldn't be able to tell them that Stalin was a war criminal, which I believed to be true. If I did, I would be put in jail.

I didn't hide the fact that I was Jewish, and my pupils knew that I had been in a concentration camp. Their reactions to hearing about my experiences were often very sweet and kind. Some of them tried to find ways to understand what I had gone through by reading books about the Holocaust or by showing me that they could relate in some way. I remember one student who came to me privately to tell me that her mother's best friend was Jewish. Another time, when I was in synagogue in Brno on one of the Jewish holidays (or, rather, what served as a synagogue after the old one had been destroyed in the war), I saw a few of my students there. I was surprised because I didn't know that they were Jewish. When I asked them why they hadn't told me, they answered, "We felt you had enough troubles in your life and we didn't want to burden you with ours."

Although they knew I had survived the concentration camp, I couldn't tell my students how I felt about those years. I taught my students about Hitler and the Nazi party – these were things that no one could deny the students had to know. But it seemed impossible for me to explain how the Nazis had created slave labour camps and killed people in gas chambers. Why did it happen? I couldn't tell them.

I did find ways to speak about my past at Auschwitz in broader terms: I spoke about injustice; I spoke about human evil; and I spoke about the persecution of innocent people. I spoke about cruelty against the helpless, like mothers and children. If you kill a child – any child, of any race, creed or religion – it is the epitome of evil. Children can't say, "We want to come into the world, we want to be born." They have no choice in the matter. This is why they need our protection, the protection of adults. As I taught my students, in quite clear terms, history proves that cruelty never wins. It cannot win.

Naturally, I had to teach these lessons in such a way that I couldn't be accused of spreading propaganda. Carefully and cleverly, I had to steer away from anything that might seem critical of the Communist regime. Since I was teaching literature, I used the themes and characters in novels to serve as metaphors in the discussion of larger issues. For example, when I taught my students about Tolstoy, whom I regard as one of the greatest writers and thinkers, I also emphasized his personal courage in spreading ideas of non-violence in the nineteenth century. Tolstoy, a pacifist, was thrown out of the Russian Orthodox Church for his belief that violence should not be used as a means of protection against evil. Although deeply religious, Tolstoy simply could not reconcile his pacifist principles with the cruelty of the Russian tsarist system. I asked my students, "What happens when a country refuses to recognize that only good will can solve problems such as intolerance and aggression? Can a country that supports human evil thrive?"

Through analyzing books like Tolstoy's *War and Peace*, I was able to teach my students lessons about human values. One of the characters in *War and Peace*, Pierre Bezukhov, for example, is portrayed as unpretentious, fun-loving and generous, but in the eyes of the Russian nobility, he is considered awkward and irrational. I asked my students to discuss whether Bezukhov is a positive or a negative character and to explain their responses. Through these discussions we got around to learning about the kind of qualities and ethics that are important.

∼

In January 1968, Alexander Dubček came to power in Czechoslovakia and began to bring in reforms that promised more freedom to the citizens of the country; they called it "socialism with a human face." That period was called the Prague Spring. Dubček freed some of the political prisoners and artists who had been jailed as dissidents; he loosened censorship in the media; and, over a period of some months, he put in place a series of plans to liberalize the government and the economy. It seemed that Soviet control over our country had ended.

The general feeling among the population was relief, optimism and hope for a better future.

Unfortunately, the relief did not last long. Perhaps the reforms were too radical or were implemented too quickly. The other communist countries in the Eastern bloc saw Dubček's reforms as a threat. On August 20, 1968, the Soviet Union and some of its allied countries – Poland, Bulgaria and Hungary – invaded Czechoslovakia. In what is known as the Warsaw Pact Invasion, Dubček was arrested and many of the reformers who were deemed anti-Soviet were detained. There were protests and there was violence. By 1969, Dubček was replaced and the reforms he had created were reversed.

Tragically, many of my colleagues who had supported the Prague Spring and its promise of freedom, or who had been critical of the Soviet occupation, were now excluded from the Communist Party and denied jobs. Even their children and their futures were put at risk. I kept in touch with my friends and still met with them, even if it had to be in secret. At the time, I seriously considered defecting to the West, to a free country. I had friends in the United States and thought to go there. But by then Czechoslovakia's borders were closed and it was too difficult.

From Communism to Canada

The idea of leaving Czechoslovakia didn't come up again until the 1980s. My daughter, Jana, had trained as a medical doctor in Czechoslovakia, graduating from Masaryk University in 1973. In 1983, Jana decided that she wanted to leave Czechoslovakia and found a way to re-certify as a medical doctor in Canada. She left that year for Toronto, Ontario and once she had completed the certification, she moved to Halifax, Nova Scotia, to begin a new life. In 1984, Jana got married and her daughter, Jolana, was born in 1986. In 1984, my son, Pavel, his wife, Klara, and their two sons, Tom and Dan, also moved to Halifax.

I still had my beautiful house in Znojmo and a life that I loved. I was comfortable, had work that I enjoyed and loving friends. Yet, when I learned that Jana was having a baby, I began to feel that my place was in Canada with my children and grandchildren. As good as my life was in Czechoslovakia, I felt it would be difficult to be there without family. After Jolana was born, I began to feel an even stronger pull to move to Canada to help Jana. She had worked so hard to build a family medical practice – I wanted to be there for her.

Once Emil and I made the decision to immigrate to Canada, we began the process of applying for legal documents and saying good-bye to our friends and our life. The entire process of getting the visas, packing and moving took about six months, and Emil and I arrived in Halifax on July 2, 1988. My granddaughter Jolana was almost two years old. Emil hadn't wanted to leave Czechoslovakia to move to Canada. He didn't speak English and didn't want to learn it, but we still managed.

Jana had found a place for us to live, where I continue to live today. It is a lovely, bright, two-floor condominium in the centre of Halifax. It was wonderful to have our own house prepared for us in an area where we could walk to everything we needed or wanted. There were, however, some challenges that initially made my life in Canada difficult. Under Czechoslovakia's communist laws we were not allowed to take with us anything except for clothing and a few household items. We also couldn't sell our home.

The most difficult situation for me, because it was an issue of moral principle, was losing my Czech teacher's pension. I had worked so very hard – I had given forty-two years of my life to the *Gymnasium* in Znojmo – but I couldn't get my retirement money when I left for Canada. I had earned that pension through my salary, and not getting that reward felt hurtful and unjust.

Fortunately, things soon changed. A little more than a year after Emil and I left, the Communist government in Czechoslovakia was overthrown in a non-violent revolution, called the Velvet Revolution, that led to the downfall of the Communist Party. They had been in power for forty-one years. Activist and playwright Václav Havel became president of the Republic of Czechoslovakia in December 1989. Among the many changes that followed from his leadership was a new law concerning teachers' pensions for those who had left the country. It took nine years and was not retroactive, but my teacher's pension was finally reinstated. I get it every month and, along with my Canada Old Age Pension, it helps me live more comfortably.

During our first years in Halifax, I took care of Jolana in our home from eight o'clock in the morning until my daughter finished work in her busy family medicine practice in the evening. When Jolana began primary school, I walked her to school in the morning and picked her up in the afternoon. At home, we read lots of stories and did activities together. Sometimes I took Jolana to friends' homes, sometimes we played in the playground very close to my apartment. In the meantime, Emil did the grocery shopping for us and helped Pavel with the bookkeeping for the three restaurants that he owned at the time. He sometimes got along by speaking German to those who could speak the language.

Aside from being with my family, the most important thing about living in Canada, for me, is freedom of speech. It did not exist in Czechoslovakia. Equally important is a stable government. In the sixty-nine years that I lived in Czechoslovakia, I had to accept censorship and lack of freedom, both of which were extremely unsettling. After all I had gone through during the war and after, living under a Communist government, the stable Canadian democracy was extremely important to me and was a tremendous relief.

In order to become more familiar with the culture, which was still foreign to me, I began watching people and observing how things worked in Canada. I tried to speak English at every opportunity and I read as many books as I could in English. I knew that for my personal happiness I would need to perfect the language because social life was important to me. Fortunately, I caught on very quickly. I made friends in a variety of ways and eventually developed the kind of rich social life that I needed. Above all, I enjoyed my freedom – the freedom of thinking, speaking and doing, without restrictions.

At the point when my English was fluent, I met a woman who invited me to join a book club. She was very well read and knew quite a lot about Czech and Russian literature. Joining the club was an excellent thing for me to do since it allowed me to become more familiar with contemporary Canadian literature, which I had never read before. The book club was not limited to Canadian books, though – we simply read good literature. The other book club members, twelve women in total, were lovely. Once a month, each of us took a turn at recommending a book and hosting the evening. That way, I too was able to share my knowledge of Russian language and literature. I remained involved with that book club for twelve years, until 2010.

When I immigrated to Canada, Jana introduced me to the synagogue that she attended regularly, the Shaar Shalom Congregation on Oxford Street in Halifax. It is affiliated with the United Synagogue of Conservative Judaism. I had grown up without any religious consciousness even though my mother and father were observant Jews. The Hebrew *Gymnasium* I had attended taught Jewish culture and some Torah, but we didn't learn about religion. In Mukačevo, women didn't participate in Jewish life. They lit Sabbath candles and prepared kosher food because that was their duty, but they had very little to do with the synagogue.

Before coming to Canada, I had found ways to be with other Jews for the Jewish holidays. There was no synagogue and no official rabbi in Znojmo, but there was a knowledgeable man in Brno who acted as rabbi on holidays, and we met in various people's homes for the services. At the Shaar Shalom in Halifax, I enjoyed the things I had always loved about attending synagogue: the beautiful prayers, the singing and the sense of spiritual community in the congregation. I also loved hearing the Hebrew language.

The people I continue to meet at the synagogue are good people and going to synagogue confirms my Jewishness. I find meaning in readings from the Torah and the interpretations offered by our rabbi. I'm also proud that my ancestors founded the Ten Commandments, which most Jews and Christians recognize as the foundation of morality. During the war, the knowledge that I gained in my study of the Torah confused me. I wanted to know why, if the Jews are God's chosen people, did I have to suffer so much? God didn't answer. I was so sad and it weighed heavily on me. When the antisemitic laws and decrees began to limit my life as a Jew – first in Mukačevo and then in Užhorod – I felt personally hurt. "Why us?" I asked.

I was afraid of being a Jew; I still sometimes feel fear in my heart. Yet, despite all that I have lived through, I never once wished that I was not Jewish. It is hard, without God, to find a sense of good, of how to live, of beauty, of friendship. It is nice to have a God, if you believe in it, and if you find it. Life is hard without God.

Epilogue: Transmitting Lessons

When my granddaughter turned twelve, she was quite independent and no longer needed me as her caregiver. This became my opportunity to make a contribution in another way. I felt I must finally speak about what I had undergone during the Holocaust. I wanted to share my knowledge and wisdom with the younger generation and to convey to them my life lessons on the evils of human cruelty and intolerance. It was more than fifty years since the end of the war and I was eighty years old.

At one point, I was asked to share my experiences in Auschwitz-Birkenau at my synagogue. Attending the talk was a professor from the University of King's College in Halifax, Dr. Dorota Glowacka, with her class of university students. The course she was teaching focused on representations of the Holocaust and the imperatives of bearing witness, remembering and confronting this terrible event. After Dr. Glowacka heard my talk, she asked me to speak to the students in her Holocaust courses at King's. With a mixture of great pleasure and considerable anxiety, I spoke to, and with, her students, and have continued to do so for the past decade.

Sharing my knowledge and experience of the Holocaust is something I feel compelled to do and it makes me feel that I am doing something good. I have a very comfortable connection with young people. In these classes, I speak about my memories of imprisonment in Birkenau, about the death march, about the trauma of recovery. As well, I speak about how this tragic time affected my life and viewpoint. I was always well received by the students, who listened to me with open hearts and showed me love and compassion. Most of them knew very little about the Holocaust and they were shocked when they heard my story. Dr. Glowacka has become a dear friend of mine.

Aside from my talks at the university, I have also been invited to speak to young schoolchildren. Without a doubt, speaking to young children is my greatest pleasure. Occasionally, I've spoken in theology departments at other universities and to various groups around Halifax.

I had been thinking about writing my memoirs since coming to Canada. I felt inspired to document my survival of the chaos of Nazi Germany. I believed that I would gain some inner satisfaction and that my heart would somehow heal if I were finally able to expose the truth and to warn people to never, ever accept evil in any guise. At one of my talks at King's in 1999, I befriended one of the students who herself felt compelled to attend the course for her own deep, personal reasons. After speaking with this woman, Carolyn Ferstman Condé, over a number of years, I felt she had the sincerity, as well as the requisite writing and technical skills, to be able to help me write this memoir.

We met, for an hour or two, once or twice a week, for more than two years to speak about my family and about my life before, during and since the Holocaust. Memoir writing is a very difficult and traumatic undertaking for a survivor of any trauma. To relive and record that trauma through writing and memory was hard – much harder than I thought it would be. I feel that I could not have written this memoir without Carolyn's assistance.

We went through a lot together and each of us felt the pain and the rewards of the experience. There were times when I felt it was too painful to remember. I didn't sleep the night before a day when we were to work together. The night after our interview, when I was

alone, I was awakened by nightmares. Willingly or not, I felt persecuted by the horrific ideas I had recalled during the day. I dreamed
that I was being attacked; I dreamed I was being physically hurt – and
I actually felt the pain. Although I wasn't bleeding, I bled. I didn't understand why. Yet, through it all, I maintained a strong sense of duty.
I had made a commitment to Carolyn and I had made a commitment
to myself. I wanted to keep my promise to both of us. That promise
carried me through the most painful times of remembering.

I still sense the courage of the women and men in the camps and
mourn the suffering of the children. We were all victims of a perverted ideology of hatred. Among the 1.5 million Jewish children killed
by Hitler's Nazis, I wonder how many little Einsteins there might have
been. How many believers in positive human values and ideals were
among those destroyed? I regard Hitler and his followers as the greatest criminals against humanity in history.

When I lecture about my life as a survivor, I generally conclude
by saying, "I know that my lecture has made you sad and I feel sad
too. I also know that you feel frightened by what I have told you. I
want to ask you to be aware of how easy it is for people to sink into a
state of intolerance and inhumanity. I don't want you to go through
what I went through. It can happen again. Witness what is happening
all over the world – people don't tell the truth, they distort historical
facts. Do not neglect your duty toward your fellow man. If we continue to be intolerant toward each other, intolerant of our differences,
and if we are unkind to others, then it can happen again."

Glossary

antisemitism Prejudice, discrimination, persecution and/or hatred against Jewish people, institutions, culture and symbols.

Appellplatz (German; the place for roll call) The area in Nazi camps where inmates had to assemble to be counted. Roll calls were part of a series of daily humiliations for prisoners, who were often made to stand completely still for hours, regardless of the weather conditions.

Auschwitz (German; in Polish, Oświęcim) A town in southern Poland approximately forty kilometres from Krakow, it is also the name of the largest complex of Nazi concentration camps that were built nearby. The Auschwitz complex contained three main camps: Auschwitz I, a slave labour camp built in May 1940; Auschwitz II-Birkenau, a death camp built in early 1942; and Auschwitz-Monowitz, a slave labour camp built in October 1942. In 1941, Auschwitz I was a testing site for usage of the lethal gas Zyklon B as a method of mass killing, which then went into wide usage. Between 1942 and 1944, transports arrived at Auschwitz-Birkenau from almost every country in Europe – hundreds of thousands from both Poland and Hungary, and thousands from France, the Netherlands, Greece, Slovakia, Bohemia and Moravia, Yugoslavia, Belgium, Italy and Norway. Between May 15 and July 8, 1944, approximately 435,000 Hungarian Jews were deported to

Auschwitz. As well, more than 30,000 people were transported there from other concentration camps. It is estimated that 1.1 million people were murdered in Auschwitz; approximately 950,000 were Jewish; 74,000 Polish; 21,000 Roma; 15,000 Soviet prisoners of war; and 10,000-15,000 other nationalities. The Auschwitz complex was liberated by the Soviet army in January 1945.

Austro-Hungarian Empire Also known as the Dual Monarchy of Austria and Hungary, ruled by the royal Habsburg family. It was successor to the Austrian Empire (1804–1867) and functioned as a dual-union state in Central Europe from 1867 to 1918. A multinational empire, the Dual Monarchy was notable for the constant political and ethnic disputes among its eleven principal national groups. Although the Empire adopted a Law of Nationalities, which officially accorded language and cultural rights to various ethnic groups, in practice, there were many inequalities in how the groups were treated. Jews were granted both citizenship rights and equal status to other minority groups, but minorities such as the Slovaks were excluded from the political sphere, whereas Czechs were accepted into government positions. The Austro-Hungarian Empire dissolved at the end of World War I and divided into the separate and independent countries of Austria, Hungary and Czechoslovakia.

Badoglio, Pietro (1871–1956) Italian general and National Fascist Party member until 1940, when he disagreed with leader Benito Mussolini's strategy and resigned as chief of staff. In July 1943, after Mussolini was removed from power, Badoglio became prime minister of Italy; he dissolved the fascist party and negotiated an armistice with the Allies in September 1943. Badoglio retired in June 1944. *See also* Mussolini, Benito.

brachah (Hebrew) Blessing.

British Mandate Palestine The area of the Middle East under British rule from 1923 to 1948, as established by the League of Nations after World War I. During that time, the United Kingdom severely restricted Jewish immigration. The Mandate area encompassed present-day Israel, Jordan, the West Bank and the Gaza Strip.

challah (Hebrew) Braided egg bread traditionally eaten on the Jewish Sabbath, Shabbat, as well as on other Jewish holidays.

Chanukah (also Hanukah; Hebrew; dedication) An eight-day festival celebrated in December to mark the victory of the Jews against foreign conquerors who desecrated the Temple in Jerusalem in the second century BCE. Traditionally, each night of the festival is marked by lighting an eight-branch candelabrum called a menorah to commemorate the rededication of the Temple and the miracle of its lamp burning for eight days without oil.

Dubček, Alexander (1921–1992) The Slovak politician who replaced Antonín Novotný as First Secretary of the Communist Party on January 5, 1968, and implemented a program of liberal reforms known as the Prague Spring. These political and economic reforms resulted in greater freedom for Czech citizens and aimed to replace the repressive, totalitarian style of communism with a more humane socialism. Dubček's April 1968 Action Program of democratic reforms included freedom of the press, freedom of speech and assembly, and greater freedom to travel. During his regime, which lasted only from January to August 1968, Dubček also federalized Czechoslovakia, creating the separate Czech Socialist Republic and Slovak Socialist Republic. The latter change was the only Dubček reform to survive the end of the Prague Spring.

Eichmann, Adolf (1906–1962) The head of the Gestapo department responsible for the implementation of the Nazis' policy of mass murder of Jews (the so-called Final Solution), Eichmann was in charge of transporting Jews to death camps in Poland. In 1942, Eichmann coordinated deportations of Jewish populations from Slovakia, the Netherlands, France and Belgium; in 1944, he was directly involved in the deportations of Jews from Hungary. After the war, Eichmann escaped from US custody and fled to Argen-

tina, where he was captured in 1960 by Israeli intelligence opera-
tives; his ensuing 1961 trial in Israel was widely and internation-
ally televised. Eichmann was sentenced to death and hanged in
May 1962.

Familienlager Theresienstadt (German; in English, Theresienstadt
Family Camp) Also known as the Czech family camp, a section
of the Birkenau "quarantine" camp where recent arrivals were
housed temporarily and that was reserved for the more than
10,000 Czech-Jewish prisoners who were deported from the
Theresienstadt camp between September and December 1943. For
approximately six months, in an effort to counteract rumours that
the Nazis were massacring Jews, the Czech Jews were accorded
privileges such as receiving parcels and writing letters, but they
were eventually subjected to the same fate as other prisoners at
Birkenau. Thousands were murdered in the gas chambers on
March 8 and 9, 1944; in July, after a selection that found only a
few thousand of the prisoners fit for forced labour, the rest of the
family camp, more than seven thousand Czech Jews, were sent to
the gas chambers. *See also* Theresienstadt.

Franco, Francisco (1892–1975) Spanish general, dictator and head of
state of Spain from 1939 to 1975. Franco, who led the Nationalists
in victory against the Republicans in the Spanish Civil War, at
first remained officially neutral and then "non-belligerent" during
World War II, but lent military support to the Axis powers. *See
also* Spanish Civil War.

Fremdarbeiter (German; foreign workers) Germany's forced labour
system during World War II, classified according to country and
"privilege." Designations included military internees (prisoners
of war); guest workers (from Scandinavian countries); civilian
workers (mostly Poles, who were badly mistreated); and Eastern
workers (from Ukraine). About twelve million Europeans were
deported to Germany over the course of the war to fulfill the need
for manual labour and the war effort; by 1944, forced labour comprised one quarter of the workforce.

Gestapo (German; abbreviation of Geheime Staatspolizei, the Secret State Police of Nazi Germany) The Gestapo were the brutal force that dealt with the perceived enemies of the Nazi regime and were responsible for rounding up European Jews for deportation to the death camps. They operated with very few legal constraints and were also responsible for issuing exit visas to the residents of German-occupied areas. A number of Gestapo members also joined the Einsatzgruppen, the mobile killing squads responsible for the roundup and murder of Jews in eastern Poland and the USSR through mass shooting operations.

Gymnasium (German) A word used throughout central and eastern Europe to mean high school.

Hasidic Judaism (from the Hebrew word *hasid*; literally, piety) An Orthodox Jewish spiritual movement founded by Rabbi Israel ben Eliezer in eighteenth-century Poland; characterized by philosophies of mysticism and focusing on joyful prayer. This movement resulted in a new kind of leader who attracted disciples as opposed to the traditional rabbis who focused on the intellectual study of Jewish law. Melody and dance have an important role in Hasidic worship. There are many different sects of Hasidic Judaism, but followers of Hasidism often wear dark, conservative clothes as well as a head covering to reflect modesty and show respect to God.

Havel, Václav (1936–2011) A playwright, poet, dissident and politician who became president of Czechoslovakia from 1989 to 1992 and the Czech Republic from 1993 to 2002. He was a key figure in both the 1968 Prague Spring attempts to bring in social and economic reforms and the 1989 Velvet Revolution that ended the Communist regime in Czechoslovakia. *See also* Velvet Revolution.

International Brigades The general name for the military units that volunteered from more than fifty countries to support the Spanish Republic by fighting against the fascist Nationalist forces during the Spanish Civil War. Between 40,000 and 60,000 volunteers, of whom approximately 1,500 were from Czechoslovakia, held either combative or non-combative roles between 1936 and 1939. *See also* Spanish Civil War.

kiddush (Hebrew; literally, sanctification) The blessing over wine that is recited on the Sabbath and other Jewish holidays. *See also* Sabbath.

kosher (Hebrew) Fit to eat according to Jewish dietary laws. Observant Jews follow a system of rules known as *kashruth* that regulates what can be eaten, how food is prepared and how meat and poultry are slaughtered. Food is kosher when it has been deemed fit for consumption according to this system of rules. There are several foods that are forbidden, most notably pork products and shellfish.

Kristallnacht (German; literally, Night of Broken Glass) A series of pogroms that took place in Germany and Austria between November 9 and 10, 1938. Over the course of twenty-four hours, ninety-one Jews were murdered, 25,000–30,000 were arrested and deported to concentration camps, two hundred synagogues were destroyed and thousands of Jewish businesses and homes were ransacked. Planned by the Nazis as a coordinated attack on the Jews of Germany and Austria, Kristallnacht is often seen as an important turning point in Hitler's policies of systematic persecution of Jews.

Läuferin (German; runner) A messenger within the Auschwitz camp system.

Masaryk, Tomáš G. (1850–1937) The founder of Czechoslovakia and first president of the country, from 1918 to 1935. Masaryk recognized minority rights and was known for his strong public opposition to antisemitism; he came to symbolize democracy to Czech citizens and has been widely honoured posthumously.

Mengele, Josef (1911–1979) The most notorious of about thirty SS garrison physicians in Auschwitz. Mengele was stationed at the camp from May 1943 to January 1945; from May 1943 to August

1944, he was the medical officer of the Birkenau "Gypsy Camp"; from August 1944 until Auschwitz was evacuated in January 1945, he became Chief Medical Officer of the main infirmary camp in Birkenau. One of the camp doctors responsible for deciding which prisoners were fit for slave labour and which were to be immediately sent to the gas chambers, Mengele was also known for conducting sadistic experiments on Jewish and Roma prisoners, especially twins.

Munich Pact An agreement signed in the early hours of September 30, 1938, by Nazi Germany, France, Britain and Italy. The Munich Pact gave Nazi Germany permission to annex the strategically important Sudeten region of Czechoslovakia in a failed attempt to appease Hitler and prevent war. Czechoslovakia was not invited to participate in the crucial conference in Munich that would determine its fate.

Mussolini, Benito (1883–1945) Prime minister of Italy from 1923 to 1943 and founder of the National Fascist Party. By 1925 Mussolini had adopted the title of "Il Duce" (leader), which referred to his position as both dictator and head of government. Mussolini gave military support to Franco's Nationalists during the Spanish Civil War and entered into an alliance with Germany in May 1939 known as the Pact of Steel. Italy officially became part of the Axis powers in September 1940. Mussolini was ousted from government in July 1943 and executed in April 1945.

Orthodox Judaism The set of beliefs and practices of Jews for whom the observance of Jewish law is closely connected to faith; it is characterized by strict religious observance of Jewish dietary laws, restrictions on work on the Sabbath and holidays, and a code of modesty in dress.

Passover (in Hebrew, Pesach) One of the major festivals of the Jewish calendar, Passover takes place over eight days in the spring. Passover commemorates the liberation and exodus of the Israelite slaves from Egypt during the reign of the Pharaoh Ramses II.

The festival begins with a lavish ritual meal called a seder during which the story of Exodus is retold through the reading of a Jewish religious text called the Haggadah. The name itself refers to the fact that God "passed over" the houses of the Jews when he set about slaying the firstborn sons of Egypt as the last of the ten plagues aimed at convincing Pharaoh to free the Jews.

peyes (Yiddish; in English, sidelocks) Among certain Orthodox Jewish communities, males refrain from cutting the hair at the edge of the face, in front of the ears. The practice of growing these distinctive locks of hair is based on a strict interpretation of the biblical verse "You shall not round off the side-growth of your head, or destroy the side-growth of your beard" (Lev. 19:27).

rabbi A Jewish teacher, scholar or leader of a congregation.

Ravensbrück The largest Nazi concentration camp created almost exclusively for women that was established in May 1939 and located about ninety kilometres north of Berlin. Throughout the war, subcamps were built in the area around Ravensbrück to serve as forced labour camps. From 1942 on, the complex served as one of the main training facilities for female SS guards. Medical experiments were carried out on the women at Ravensbrück and in early 1945 the SS built a gas chamber, where between 5,000 and 6,000 prisoners were murdered. More than 100,000 women prisoners from all over Nazi-occupied Europe had passed through Ravensbrück before the Soviets liberated the camp on April 29-30, 1945. Approximately 50,000 women died in the camp.

Red Cross A humanitarian organization founded in 1863 to protect the victims of war. During World War II the Red Cross provided assistance to prisoners of war by distributing food parcels and monitoring the situation in POW camps, and also provided medical attention to wounded soldiers and civilians. Today, in addition to the international body, the International Committee of the Red Cross (ICRC), there are national Red Cross and Red Crescent societies in almost every country in the world.

Roma Also known as Romani. An ethnic group primarily located in central and eastern Europe. The Roma were commonly referred to as Gypsies in the past, a term now generally considered to be derogatory, and they have often lived on the fringes of society and been subject to persecution. During the Holocaust, which the Roma refer to in Romani as the *Porajmos* – the devouring – they were stripped of their citizenship under the Nuremberg Laws and were targeted for death under Hitler's race policies. The estimation of how many Roma were killed varies widely and has been difficult to document – estimations generally range between 200,000 and one million.

Russian Revolution The 1917 February and October revolutions that led to the dissolution of the autocratic tsarist regime and the creation of a Communist government, respectively. The provisional government established after the February revolt was defeated by the Bolsheviks in October. The Bolshevik government – also referred to as the "reds" – was subsequently challenged by the "whites" or anti-Bolsheviks, which resulted in a five-year civil war.

Sabbath (in Hebrew, Shabbat; in Yiddish, Shabbes, Shabbos) The weekly day of rest beginning Friday at sunset and ending Saturday at sundown, ushered in by the lighting of candles on Friday night and the recitation of blessings over wine and challah (egg bread); a day of celebration as well as prayer, it is customary to eat three festive meals, attend synagogue services and refrain from doing any work or travelling.

Shema Yisrael (Hebrew; in English, "Hear, O Israel") The first two words of a section of the Torah and an extremely important prayer in Judaism. The full verse is "Hear, O Israel: the Lord is our God, the Lord is One" and refers to faith and loyalty in one God, which is the essence of Judaism. The *Shema* prayer comprises three verses in the Torah and observant Jews recite the *Shema* daily, in the morning, evening, and at bedtime.

Sonderkommando (German; special unit) Concentration camp prisoners charged with removing corpses from the gas chambers, loading them into the crematoria and disposing of the remains.

Spanish Civil War (1936–1939) The war in Spain between the military – supported by Conservative, Catholic and fascist elements, together called the Nationalists – and the Republican government. Sparked by an initial coup that failed to win a decisive victory, the country was plunged into a bloody civil war. It ended when the Nationalists, under the leadership of General Francisco Franco, marched into Madrid. During the civil war, the Nationalists received aid from both Fascist Italy and Nazi Germany, and the Republicans received aid from volunteers worldwide. *See also* Franco, Francisco; International Brigades.

SS (abbreviation of Schutzstaffel; Defence Corps) The SS was established in 1925 as Adolf Hitler's elite corps of personal bodyguards. Under the direction of Heinrich Himmler, its membership grew from 280 in 1929 to 50,000 when the Nazis came to power in 1933, and to nearly a quarter of a million on the eve of World War II. The SS was comprised of the Allgemeine-SS (General SS) and the Waffen-SS (Armed, or Combat SS). The General SS dealt with policing and the enforcement of Nazi racial policies in Germany and the Nazi-occupied countries. An important unit within the SS was the Reichssicherheitshauptamt (RSHA, the Central Office of Reich Security), whose responsibility included the Gestapo (Geheime Staatspolizei). The SS ran the concentration and death camps, with all their associated economic enterprises, and also fielded its own Waffen-SS military divisions, including some recruited from the occupied countries. *See also* Gestapo.

Stalin, Joseph (1878–1953) The leader of the Soviet Union from 1924 until his death in 1953. Born Joseph Vissarionovich Dzhugashvili, he changed his name to Stalin (literally: man of steel) in 1903. He was a staunch supporter of Lenin, taking control of the Communist Party upon Lenin's death. Very soon after acquiring leadership of the Communist Party, Stalin ousted rivals, killed opponents in purges, and effectively established himself as a dictator. During the late 1930s, Stalin commenced "The Great Purge," during which he targeted and disposed of elements within the Communist Party that he deemed to be a threat to the stability of the Soviet Union. These purges extended to both military and civilian society, and millions of people were incarcerated or exiled to harsh labour camps. During the war and in the immediate postwar period, many Jews in Poland viewed Stalin as the leader of the country that liberated them and saved them from death at the hands of the Nazis. At the time, many people were unaware of the extent of Stalin's own murderous policies. After World War II, Stalin set up Communist governments controlled by Moscow in many Eastern European states bordering and close to the USSR, and instituted antisemitic campaigns and purges.

Star of David (in Hebrew, *Magen David*) The six-pointed star that is the ancient and most recognizable symbol of Judaism. During World War II, Jews in Nazi-occupied areas were frequently forced to wear a badge or armband with the Star of David on it as an identifying mark of their lesser status and to single them out as targets for persecution.

Torah (Hebrew) The Five Books of Moses (the first five books of the Bible), also called the Pentateuch. The Torah is the core of Jewish scripture, traditionally believed to have been given to Moses on Mount Sinai. In Christianity it is referred to as the "Old Testament."

Velvet Revolution (November 17–December 29, 1989) The peaceful transition from communism to a parliamentary republic in Czechoslovakia. Government protests broke out on November 17, International Students' Day in Prague, and continued to grow in strength and numbers, culminating in the resignation of the Communist Party on November 24 and the fall of communism. Subsequently, playwright and activist Václav Havel was elected as president on December 29, 1989, marking the end of the revolution. *See also* Havel, Václav.

yeshiva (Hebrew) A Jewish educational institution in which religious texts such as the Torah and Talmud are studied.

Yiddish A language derived from Middle High German with elements of Hebrew, Aramaic, Romance and Slavic languages, and written in Hebrew characters. Spoken by Jews in east-central Europe for roughly a thousand years from the tenth century to the mid-twentieth century, it was still the most common language among European Jews until the outbreak of World War II. There are similarities between Yiddish and contemporary German.

Zionism A movement promoted by the Viennese Jewish journalist Theodor Herzl, who argued in his 1896 book *Der Judenstaat* (The Jewish State) that the best way to resolve the problem of anti-semitism and persecution of Jews in Europe was to create an independent Jewish state in the historic Jewish homeland of Biblical Israel. Zionists also promoted the revival of Hebrew as a Jewish national language.

Photographs

Helena Jockel, 1948.

1 Helena's sister Agneszka (Agi) with her family after the war. From left to right:
   Agi; daughter Vera; her husband, Josef Soffer; and daughter Ruzena.
2 Agi, date unknown.
3 Agi with her great-granddaughter, Sofinka, circa 2004.
4 Helena on a visit to Agi and her family in Znojmo. From left to right: Agi with
   her great-grandson, David, on her lap; Agi's granddaughter Vendulka; and Helena. Znojmo, 1999.

1

2

1 The gate to the Mukačevo ghetto, 1944.

2 The brickyard where the Jews of Mukačevo were assembled before being deported to Auschwitz.

(Photos courtesy of Ghetto Fighters' House Museum.)

Helena and her husband, Emil Jockel, at the Spa Marianske Lazne Film Festival, 1948. Photo courtesy of the United States Holocaust Memorial Museum.

1

2

1 The Hebrew *Gymnasium* in Mukačevo, where Helena went to school. Photo
   courtesy of the United States Holocaust Memorial Museum.
2 Helena (front row, holding a handbag) with the faculty of the *Gymnasium* in
   Znojmo, where she taught for more than forty years. Date unknown.

1

2

3

1 Emil and Helena with their children, Pavel (left) and Jana (right), in Jubilejni
   Park. Znojmo, circa 1955.
2 Jana and Emil, circa 1956.
3 Helena with Jana, age seven, and Pavel, age four.

Helena Jockel, 1956.

1 Helena with her daughter, Jana, and granddaughter, Jolana, in Halifax in the 1990s.
2 Helena's son, Pavel, daughter-in-law, Klara, and grandsons Tom (front) and Dan.

Helena and Emil preparing strawberries for jam. Halifax, 1992.

Index

The Azrieli Foundation was established in 1989 to realize and extend the philanthropic vision of David J. Azrieli, C.M., C.Q., M.Arch. The Foundation's mission is to support a wide spectrum of initiatives in education and research. The Azrieli Foundation is an active supporter of programs in the fields of Jewish education, the education of architects, scientific and medical research, and education in the arts. The Azrieli Foundation's many well-known initiatives include: the Holocaust Survivor Memoirs Program, which collects, preserves, publishes and distributes the written memoirs of survivors in Canada; the Azrieli Institute for Educational Empowerment, an innovative program successfully working to keep at-risk youth in school; and the Azrieli Fellows Program, which promotes academic excellence and leadership on the graduate level at Israeli universities.